# The Acts of the Disposition with the Heresiarch Manes

# The Acts of the Disposition with the Heresiarch Manes

## Archelaus

# The Acts of the Disposition with the Heresiarch Manes

© Lighthouse Publishing 2024

Written by: Archelaus, Bishop of Carrhae (AD 200 - 245)
Translated by: Rev. S. D. F. Salmond, M.A..(1838 – 1905)
Updated into Modern U.S English: A.M. Overett (b.1960)

All rights reserved. Without limiting the rights under copyright reserved above, no part of this publication may be reproduced, stored in a retrieval system, or transmitted, in any form or by any means (electronic, mechanical, photocopying, recording or otherwise), without the prior written permission of the copyright owner of this book.

Published by
Lighthouse Publishing
SAN 257-4330
228 Freedom Parkway
Hoschton, GA 30548
United States of America

www.lighthousechristianpublishing.com

Introductory Notice
to
Archelaus.

[a.d. 277.] The Manichæan heresy, which was destined to operate so terribly against the Church and the purity of the Gospel, encountered its earliest successful antagonism in the *Thebaid*; and I have not doubted the wisdom of prefixing this *Disputation* to the veritable name and work of Alexander of Lycopolis, as important to the complete history of the great Alexandrian school. The Edinburgh translator of this work regards it as an "authentic relic of antiquity," in spite of Beausobre, who treats it as a romance. I have forced myself, in this republication, to reject no theory of the Edinburgh collaborators to which I have not been able to give as much critical attention, at least, as they have evidently bestowed upon their work. It seems to me a well-sustained presumption that the work is fundamentally real, and Dr. Neander admits its base of fact. It is useful, at any rate, in its form and place, as here presented, and so much may be inferred from the following:—

Translator's Introductory Notice.

A certain memorable Disputation, which was conducted by a bishop of the name of Archelaus with the heretic Manes, is mentioned by various writers of an early date. What professes to be an account of that Disputation has come down to us in a form mainly Latin, but with parts in Greek. A considerable portion of this Latin version was published by Valesius in his edition of Socrates and Sozomen, and subsequently by others in greater completeness, and with the addition of the Greek fragments. There seems to be a difference among the

# The Acts of the Disposition with the Heresiarch Manes

ancient authorities cited above as to the person who committed these *Acts* to writing. Epiphanius and Jerome take it to have been Archelaus himself, while Heraclianus, bishop of Chalcedon, represents it to have been a certain person named Hegemonius. In Photius there is a statement to the effect that this Heraclianus, in confuting the errors of the Manichæans, made use of certain Acts of the Disputation of Bishop Archelaus with Manes which were written by Hegemonius. And there are various passages in the *Acts* themselves which appear to confirm the opinion of Heraclianus. Zacagnius, however, thinks that this is but an apparent discrepancy, which is easily reconciled on the supposition that the book was first composed by Archelaus himself in Syriac, and afterwards edited, with certain amendments and additions, by Hegemonius. That the work was written originally in Syriac is clear, not only from the express testimony of Jerome, but also from internal evidence, and specially from the explanations offered now and again of the use of Greek equivalents. It is uncertain who was the author of the Greek version; and we can only conjecture that Hegemonius, in publishing a new edition, may also have undertaken a translation into the tongue which would secure a much larger audience than the original Syriac. But that this Greek version, by whomsoever accomplished, dates from the very earliest period, is proved by the excerpts given in Epiphanius. As to the Latin interpretation itself, all that we can allege is, that it must in all probability have been published after Jerome's time, who might reasonably be expected to have made some allusion to it if it was extant in his day; and before the seventh century, because, in quoting the Scriptures, it does not follow the Vulgate edition, which was received generally throughout the West by that period. That the Latin translator must have had before him, not the Syriac, but the Greek copy, is also manifest, not only from the general idiomatic character of the rendering, but also from many nicer indications.

The precise designation of the seat of the bishopric of Archelaus has been the subject of considerable diversity of opinion. Socrates and Epiphanius record that Archelaus was bishop *of Caschar*, or *Caschara*. Epiphanius, however, does not keep consistently by that scription. In the opening sentence of the *Acts* themselves it appears as Carchar. Now we know that there were at least two towns of the name of Carcha: for the anonymous Ravenna geographer tells us that there was a place of that name in Arabia Felix; and Ammianus Marcellinus mentions another beyond the Tigris, within the Persian dominion. The clear statements, however, to the effect that the locality of the bishopric of Archelaus was in Mesopotamia, make it impossible that either of these two towns could have been the seat of his rule. Besides this, in the third chapter of the *Acts* themselves we find the name *Charra* occurring; and hence Zacagnius and others have concluded that the place actually intended is the scriptural *Charran*, or Haran, in Mesopotamia, which is also written *Charra* in Paulus Diaconus, and that the form Carchar or Carchara was either a mere error of the transcribers, or the vulgar provincial designation. It must be added, however, that Neander allows this to be only a very uncertain conjecture, while others hold that *Caschar* is the most probable scription, and that the town is one altogether different from the ancient Haran.

The date of the Disputation itself admits of tolerably exact settlement. Epiphanius, indeed, says that

# The Acts of the Disposition with the Heresiarch Manes

Manes fled into Mesopotamia in the ninth year of the reign of Valerianus and Gallienus, and that the discussion with Archelaus took place about the same time. This would carry the date back to about 262 a.d. But this statement, although he is followed in it by Petrus Siculus and Photius, is inconsistent with the specification of times which he makes in dealing with the error of the Manichæans in his book *On the Heresies*. From the 37th chapter of the *Acts*, however, we find that the Disputation took place, not when Gallienus, but when Probus held the empire, and that is confirmed by Cyril of Jerusalem. The exact year becomes also clearer from Eusebius, who seems to indicate the second year of the reign of Probus as the time when the Manichæan heresy attained general publicity—*Secundo anno Probi...insana Manichæorum hæresis in commune humani generis malum exorta*; and from Leo Magnus, who in his second *Discourse on Pentecost* also avers that Manichæus became notorious in the consulship of Probus and Paulinus. And as this consulship embraced part of the first and part of the second years of the empire of Probus, the Disputation itself would thus be fixed as occurring in the end of a.d. 277 or the beginning of 278, or, according to the precise calculation of Zacagnius, between July and December of the year 277.

That the *Acts* of this Disputation constitute an authentic relic of antiquity, seems well established by a variety of considerations. Epiphanius, for instance, writing about the year a.d. 376, makes certain excerpts from them which correspond satisfactorily with the extant Latin version. Socrates, again, whose *Ecclesiastical History* dates about 439, mentions these *Acts*, and acknowledges that he drew the materials for his account of the Manichæan heresy from them. The book itself, too, offers not a few evidences of its own antiquity and authenticity. The enumeration given of the various heretics who had appeared up to the time of Archelaus, the mention of his presence at the siege of the city, and the allusions to various customs, have all been pressed into that service, as may be seen in detail in the elaborate dissertation prefixed by Zacagnius in his *Collectanea Monumentorum Ecclesiæ Græcæ*. At the same time, it is very evident that the work has come down to us in a decidedly imperfect form. There are, for example, arguments by Manes and answers by Archelaus recorded in Cyril which are not contained in our Latin version at all. And there are not a few notes of discrepancy and broken connections in the composition itself, which show that the manuscripts must have been defective, or that the Latin translator took great liberties with the Greek text, or that the Greek version itself did not faithfully reproduce the original Syriac. On the historical character of the work Neander expresses himself thus: "These *Acts* manifestly contain an ill-connected narrative, savoring in no small degree of the romantic. Although there is some truth at the bottom of it—as, for instance, in the statement of doctrine there is much that wears the appearance of truth, and is confirmed also by its agreement with other representations: still the Greek author seems, from ignorance of Eastern languages and customs, to have introduced a good deal that is untrue, by bringing in and confounding together discordant stories through an uncritical judgment and exaggeration."

# The Acts of the Disputation with the Heresiarch Manes.

1. The true Thesaurus; to wit, the Disputation conducted in Carchar, a city of Mesopotamia, before Manippus and Ægialeus and Claudius and Cleobolus, who acted as judges. In this city of Mesopotamia there was a certain man, Marcellus by name, who was esteemed as a person worthy of the highest honor for his manner of life, his pursuits, and his lineage, and not less so for his discretion and his nobility of character: he was possessed also of abundant means; and, what is most important of all, he feared God with the deepest piety, and gave ear always with due reverence to the things which were spoken of Christ. In short, there was no good quality lacking in that man, and hence it came to pass that he was held in the greatest regard by the whole city; while, on the other hand, he also made an ample return for the good-will of his city by his munificent and oft-repeated acts of liberality in bestowing on the poor, relieving the afflicted, and giving help to the distressed. But let it suffice us to have said thus much, lest by the weakness of our words we rather take from the man's virtues than adduce what is worthy of their splendor. I shall come, therefore, to the task which forms my subject. On a certain occasion, when a large body of captives were offered to the bishop Archelaus by the soldiers who held the camp in that place, their numbers being some seven thousand seven hundred, he was harassed with the keenest anxiety on account of the large sum of money which was demanded by the soldiers as the price of the prisoners' deliverance. And as he could not conceal his solicitude, all aflame for the religion and the fear of God, he at length hastened to

Marcellus, and explained to him the importance and difficulty of the case. And when that pattern of piety, Marcellus, heard his narration, without the least delay he went into his house, and provided the price demanded for the prisoners, according to the value set upon them by those who had led them captive; and unlocking the treasures of his goods, he at once distributed the gifts of piety among the soldiers, without any severe consideration of number or distinction, so that they seemed to be presents rather than purchase-moneys. And those soldiers were filled with wonder and admiration at the grandeur of the man's piety and munificence, and were struck with amazement, and felt the force of this example of pity; so that very many of them were added to the faith of our Lord Jesus Christ, and threw off the belt of military service, while others withdrew to their camp, taking scarcely a fourth part of the ransom, and the rest made their departure without receiving even so much as would defray the expenses of the way.

2. Marcellus, as might well be expected, was exceedingly gratified by these incidents; and summoning one of the prisoners, by name Cortynius, he inquired of him the cause of the war, and by what chance it was that they were overcome and bound with the chains of captivity. And the person addressed, on obtaining liberty to speak, began to express himself in these terms: "My lord Marcellus, we believe in the living God alone. And we have a custom of such a nature as I shall now describe, which has descended to us by the tradition of our brethren *in the faith*, and has been regularly observed by us up to the present day. The practice is, that every year we go out beyond the bounds of the city, in company with our wives and children, and offer up supplications to the only and

invisible God, praying Him to send us rains for our fields and crops. Now, when we were celebrating this observance at the usual time and in the wonted manner, evening surprised us as we lingered there, and were still fasting. Thus we were feeling the pressure of two of the most trying things men have to endure,—namely, fasting and want of sleep. But about midnight sleep enviously and inopportunely crept upon us, and with necks drooping and unstrung, and heads hanging down, it made our faces strike against our knees. Now this took place because the time was at hand when by the judgment of God we were to pay the penalty proper to our deserts, whether it might be that we were offenders in ignorance, or whether it might be that with the consciousness of wrong we nevertheless had not given up our sin. Accordingly at that hour a multitude of soldiers suddenly surrounded us, supposing us, as I judge, to have lodged ourselves in ambush there, and to be persons with full experience and skill in fighting battles; and without making any exact inquiry into the cause of our gathering there, they threatened us with war, not in word, but at once by the sword. And though we were men who had never learned to do injury to anyone, they wounded us pitilessly with their missiles, and thrust us through with their spears, and cut our throats with their swords. Thus they slew, indeed, about one thousand and three hundred men of our number, and wounded other five hundred. And when the day broke clearly, they carried off the survivors amongst us as prisoners here, and that, too, in a way showing their utter want of pity for us. For they drove us before their horses, spurring us on by blows from their spears, and impelling us forward by making the horses' heads press upon us. And those who had sufficient powers of endurance did indeed hold out; but very many fell down before the face of their cruel masters, and breathed out their life there; and mothers, with arms wearied, and utterly powerless with their burdens, and distracted by the threats of those behind them, suffered the little ones that were hanging on their breasts to fall to the ground; while all those on whom old age had come were sinking, one after the other, to the earth, overcome with their toils, and exhausted by want of food. The proud soldiers nevertheless enjoyed this bloody spectacle of men continually perishing, as if it had been a kind of entertainment, while they saw some stretched on the soil in hopeless prostration, and beheld others, worn out by the fierce fires of thirst and with the bands of their tongues utterly parched, lose the power of speech, and beheld others with eyes ever glancing backwards, groaning over the fate of their dying little ones, while these, again, were constantly appealing to their most unhappy mothers with their cries, and the mothers themselves, driven frantic by the severities of the robbers, responded with their lamentations, which indeed was the only thing they could do freely. And those of them whose hearts were most tenderly bound up with their offspring chose voluntarily to meet the same premature fate of death with their children; while those, on the other hand, who had some capacity of endurance were carried off prisoners here with us. Thus, after the lapse of three days, during which time we had never been allowed to take any rest, even in the night, we were conveyed to this place, in which what has now taken place after these occurrences is better known to yourself."

3. When Marcellus, the man of consummate piety, had heard this recital, he burst into a flood of tears,

## The Acts of the Disposition with the Heresiarch Manes

touched with pity for misfortunes so great and so various. But making no delay, he at once prepared victuals for the sufferers, and did service with his own hand for the wearied; in this imitating our father Abraham the patriarch, who, when he entertained the angels hospitably on a certain occasion, did not content himself with merely giving the order to his slaves to bring a calf from the herd, but did himself, though advanced in years, go and place it on his shoulders and fetch it in, and did with his own hand prepare food, and set it before the angels. So Marcellus, in discharge of a similar office, directed them to be seated as his guests in companies of ten; and when the seven hundred tables were all provided, he refreshed the whole body of the captives with great delight, so that those who had strength to survive what they had been called to endure, forgot their toils, and became oblivious of all their ills. When, however, they had reached the fifteenth day, and while Marcellus was still liberally supplying all things needful for the prisoners, it seemed good to him that they should all be put in possession of the means of returning to their own parts, with the exception of those who were detained by the attention which their wounds demanded; and providing the proper remedies for these, he instructed the rest to depart to their own country and friends. And even to all these charities Marcellus added yet larger deeds of piety. For with a numerous band of his own dependents he went to look after the burying of the bodies of those who had perished on the march; and for as many of these as he could discover, of whatsoever condition, he secured the sepulture which was meet for them. And when this service was completed he returned to Charra, and gave permission to the wounded to return to their native country when their health was sufficiently restored, providing also most liberal supplies for their use on their journey. And truly the estimate of this deed made a magnificent addition to *the repute of* the other noble actions of Marcellus; for through that whole territory the fame of the piety of Marcellus spread so grandly, that large numbers of men belonging to various cities were inflamed with the intense desire to see and become acquainted with the man, and most especially those persons who had not had occasion to bear penury before,—to all of whom this remarkable man, following the example of a Marcellus of old, furnished aid most indulgently, so that they all declared that there was no one of more illustrious piety than this man. Yea, all the widows, too, who were believers in the Lord had recourse to him, while the imbecile also could reckon on obtaining at his hand most certain help to meet their circumstances; and the orphaned, in like manner, were all supported by him, so that his house was declared to be the hospice for the stranger and the indigent. And above all this, he retained in a remarkable and singular measure his devotion to the faith, building up his own heart upon the rock that shall not be moved.

4. Accordingly, as this man's fame was becoming always the more extensively diffused throughout different localities, and when it had now penetrated even beyond the river Stranga, the honorable report of his name was carried into the territory of Persia. In this country dwelt a person called Manes, who, when this man's repute had reached him, deliberated largely with himself as to how he might entangle him in the snares of his doctrine, hoping that Marcellus might be made an upholder of his dogma. For he reckoned that he might make himself master of the whole province if he could only first attach

such a man to himself. In this project, however, his mind was agitated with the doubt whether he should at once repair in person to the man, or first attempt to get at him by letter; for he was afraid lest, by any sudden and unexpected introduction of himself upon the scene some mischance might possibly befall him. At last, in obedience to a subtler policy, he resolved to write; and calling to him one of his disciples, by name Turbo, who had been instructed by Addas, he handed to him an epistle, and bade him depart and convey it to Marcellus. This adherent accordingly received the letter, and carried it to the person to whom he had been commissioned by Manes to deliver it, overtaking the whole journey within five days. The abovementioned Turbo, indeed, used great expedition on this journey, in the course of which he also underwent very considerable exertion and trouble. For whenever he arrived, as a traveler in foreign parts, at a hospice,—and these were inns which Marcellus himself had supplied in his large hospitality,—on his being asked by the keepers of these hostels whence he came, and who he was, or by whom he had been sent, he used to reply: "I belong to the district of Mesopotamia, but I come at present from Persis, having been sent by Manichæus, a master among the Christians." But they were by no means ready to welcome a name unknown to them, and were wont sometimes to thrust Turbo out of their inns, refusing him even the means of getting water for drinking purposes. And as he had to bear daily things like these, and things even worse than these, at the hands of those persons in the several localities who had charge of the mansions and hospices, unless he had at last shown that he was conveying letters to Marcellus, Turbo would have met the doom of death in his travels.

5. On receiving the epistle, then, Marcellus opened it, and read it in the presence of Archelaus, the bishop of the place. And the following is a copy of what it contained:—

Manichæus, an apostle of Jesus Christ, and all the saints who are with me, and the virgins, to Marcellus, my beloved son: Grace, mercy, and peace be with you from God the Father, and from our Lord Jesus Christ; and may the right hand of light preserve you safe from this present evil world, and from its calamities, and from the snares of the wicked one. Amen. I was exceedingly delighted to observe the love cherished by you, which truly is of the largest measure. But I was distressed at your faith, which is not in accordance with the right standard. Wherefore, deputed as I am to seek the elevation of the race of men, and sparing, as I do, those who have given themselves over to deceit and error, I have considered it needful to dispatch this letter to you, with a view, in the first place, to the salvation of your own soul, and in the second place also to that of the souls of those who are with you, so as to secure you against dubious opinions, and specially against notions like those in which the guides of the simpler class of minds indoctrinate their subjects, when they allege that good and evil have the same original subsistence, and when they posit the same beginning for them, without making any distinction or discrimination between light and darkness, and between the good and the evil or worthless, and between the inner man and the outer, as we have stated before, and without ceasing to mix up and confound together the one with the other. But, O my son, refuse thou thus thoughtlessly to identify these two things in the irrational and foolish fashion common to the mass of men, and ascribe no such confusion to the

God of goodness. For these men refer the beginning and the end and the paternity of these ills to God Himself,—"whose end is near a curse." For they do not believe the word spoken by our Savior and Lord Jesus Christ Himself in the Gospels, namely, that "a good tree cannot bring forth evil fruit, neither can a corrupt tree bring forth good fruit." And how they can be bold enough to call God the maker and contriver of Satan and his wicked deeds, is a matter of great amazement to me. Yea, would that even this had been all the length to which they had gone with their silly efforts, and that they had not declared that the only-begotten Christ, who has descended from the bosom of the Father, is the son of a certain woman, Mary, and born of blood and flesh and the varied impurities proper to women! Howbeit, neither to write too much in this epistle, nor to trespass at too great length upon your good nature,—and all the more so that I have no natural gift of eloquence,—I shall content myself with what I have said. But you will have full knowledge of the whole subject when I am present with you, if indeed you still continue to care for your own salvation. For I do not "cast a snare upon anyone," as is done by the less thoughtful among the mass of men. Think of what I say, most honorable son.

6. On reading this epistle, Marcellus, with the kindest consideration, attended hospitably to the needs of the bearer of the letter. Archelaus, on the other hand, did not receive very pleasantly the matters which were read, but "gnashed with his teeth like a chained lion," impatient to have the author of the epistle given over to him. Marcellus, however, counseled him to be at peace; promising that he would himself take care to secure the man's presence. And accordingly, Marcellus resolved to

send an answer to what had been written to him, and indited an epistle containing the following statements:—

Marcellus, a man of distinction, to Manichæus, who has made himself known to me by his epistle, greeting.

An epistle written by you has come to my hand, and I have received Turbo with my wonted kindness; but the meaning of your letter I have by no means apprehended, and may not do so unless you give us your presence, and explain its contents in detail in the way of conversation, as you have offered to do in the epistle itself. Farewell.

This letter he sealed and handed to Turbo, with instructions to deliver it to the person from whom he had already conveyed a similar document. The messenger, however, was extremely reluctant to return to his master, being mindful of what he had to endure on the journey, and begged that another person should be dispatched in his stead, refusing to go back to Manes, or to have any intercourse whatever with him again. But Marcellus summoned one of his young men, Callistus by name, and directed him to proceed to the place. Without any loss of time this young man set out promptly on his journey thither; and after the lapse of three days he came to Manes, whom he found in a certain fort, that of Arabion to wit, and to whom he presented the epistle. On perusing it, he was glad to see that he had been invited by Marcellus; and without delay he undertook the journey; yet he had a presentiment that Turbo's failure to return boded no good, and proceeded on his way to Marcellus, not, as it were, without serious reflections. Turbo, for his part, was not at all thinking of leaving the house of Marcellus; neither did he omit any opportunity of conversing with Archelaus the bishop. For both these parties were very diligently engaged in investigating the practices of Manichæus, being desirous of knowing who he was and whence he came, and what was his manner of discourse. And he, Turbo, accordingly, gave a lucid account of the whole position, narrating and expounding the terms of his faith in the following manner:—

If you are desirous of being instructed in the faith of Manes by me, attend to me for a short space. That man worships two deities, unoriginated, self-existent, eternal, opposed the one to the other. Of these he represents the one as good, and the other as evil, and assigns the name of *Light* to the former, and that of *Darkness* to the latter. He alleges also that the soul in men is a portion of the *light*, but that the body and the formation of matter are parts of the *darkness*. He maintains, further, that a certain commingling or blending has been effected between the two in the manner about to be stated, the following analogy being used as an illustration of the same; to wit, that their relations may be likened to those of two kings in conflict with each other, who are antagonists from the beginning, and have their own positions, each in his due order. And so he holds that the darkness passed without its own boundaries, and engaged in a similar contention with the light; but that the good Father then, perceiving that the darkness had come to sojourn on His earth, put forth from Himself a power which is called the Mother of Life; and that this power thereupon put forth from itself *the first man, and* the five elements. And these five elements are wind, light, water, fire, and matter. Now this primitive man, being endued with these, and thereby equipped, as it were, for war, descended to these lower parts, and made war against the darkness. But the princes of the darkness, waging war in turn against him, consumed that portion of his panoply which is the soul. Then was that *first man* grievously injured there underneath by the darkness; and had it not been that the Father heard his prayers, and sent a second power, which was also put forth from Himself and was called the *living Spirit*, and came down and gave him the right hand, and brought him up again out of the grasp of the darkness, that *first man* would, in those ancient times, have been in peril of absolute overthrow. From that time, consequently, he left the soul beneath. And for this reason the Manichæans, if they meet each other, give the right hand, in token of their having been saved from darkness; for he holds that the heresies have their seat all in the darkness. Then the living Spirit created the world; and bearing in himself three other powers, he came down and brought off the princes, and settled them in the firmament, which is their body, (though it is called) the sphere. Then, again, the living Spirit created the luminaries, which are fragments of the soul, and he made them thus to move round and round the firmament; and again he created the earth in its eight species. And the Omophorus sustains the burden thereof beneath; and when he is wearied with bearing it he trembles, and in that manner becomes the cause of a quaking of the earth in contravention of its determinate times. On account of this the good Father sent His Son forth from His own bosom into the heart of the earth, and into these lowest parts of it, in order to secure for him the correction befitting him. And whenever an earthquake occurs, he is either trembling under his weariness, or is shifting his burden from one shoulder to the other. Thereafter, again, the matter also of itself produced growths; and when these were carried off as spoil on the part of some of the princes, he summoned together all the foremost of the princes, and took from all of them individually power after power, and made up the man who is after the image of that *first man*, and united the soul (with these powers) in him. This is the account of the manner in which his constitution was planned.

8. But when the living Father perceived that the soul was in tribulation in the body, being full of mercy and compassion, He sent His own beloved Son for the salvation of the soul. For this, together with the matter of Omophorus, was the reason of His sending Him. And the Son came and transformed Himself into the likeness of man, and manifested Himself to men as a man, while yet He was not a man, and men supposed that He was begotten. Thus He came and prepared the work which was to effect the salvation of the souls, and with that object constructed an instrument with twelve urns, which is made to revolve by the sphere, and draws up with it the souls of the dying. And the greater luminary receives these souls, and purifies them with its rays, and then passes them over to the moon; and in this manner the moon's disc, as it is designated by us, is filled up. For he says that these two luminaries are ships or passage-boats. Then, if the moon becomes full, it ferries its passengers across toward the east wind, and thereby effects its own waning in getting itself delivered of its freight. And in this manner it goes on making the passage across, and again discharging its freight of souls drawn up by the urns, until it saves its own proper portion of the souls. Moreover, he maintains that every soul, yea, every living creature that moves, partakes of the substance of the good Father. And accordingly, when the moon delivers over its freight of souls to the æons of the Father, they abide there in that

pillar of glory, which is called the perfect air. And this air is a pillar of light, for it is filled with the souls that are being purified. Such, moreover, is the agency by which the souls are saved. But the following, again, is the cause of men's dying: A certain virgin, fair in person, and beautiful in attire, and of most persuasive address, aims at making spoil of the princes that have been borne up and crucified on the firmament by the living Spirit; and she appears as a comely female to the princes, but as a handsome and attractive young man to the princesses. And the princes, when they look on her in her splendid figure, are smitten with love's sting; and as they are unable to get possession of her, they burn fiercely with the flame of amorous desire, and lose all power of reason. While they thus pursue the virgin, she disappears from view. Then the great prince sends forth from himself the clouds, with the purpose of bringing darkness on the whole world, in his anger. And then, if he feels grievously oppressed, his exhaustion expresses itself in perspiration, just as a man sweats under toil; and this sweat of his forms the rain. At the same time also the harvest-prince, if he too chances to be captivated by the virgin, scatters pestilence on the whole earth, with the view of putting men to death. Now this body (of man) is also called a *cosmos*, i.e., a microcosm, in relation to the great *cosmos*, i.e., the macrocosm of the universe; and all men have roots which are linked beneath with those above. Accordingly, when this prince is captivated by the virgin's charms, he then begins to cut the roots of men; and when their roots are cut, then pestilence commences to break forth, and in that manner they die. And if he shakes the upper parts of the root mightily, an earthquake bursts, and follows as the consequence of the commotion to which the Omophorus is subjected. This is the explanation of (the phenomenon of) death.

9. I shall explain to you also how it is that the soul is transfused into five bodies. First of all, in this process some small portion of it is purified; and then it is transfused into the body of a dog, or a camel, or some other animal. But if the soul has been guilty of homicide, it is translated into the body of the celephi; and if it has been found to have engaged in cutting; it is made to pass into the *body of the* dumb. Now these are the designations of the soul,—namely, intelligence, reflection, prudence, consideration, reasoning. Moreover, the reapers who reap are likened to the princes who have been in darkness from the beginning, since they consumed somewhat of the panoply of the first man. On this account there is a necessity for these to be translated into hay, or beans, or barley, or corn, or vegetables, in order that in these forms they, in like manner, may be reaped and cut. And again, if any one eats bread, he must needs also become bread and be eaten. If one kills a chicken, he will be a chicken himself. If one kills a mouse, he will also become a mouse himself. If, again, one is wealthy in this world, it is necessary that, on quitting the tabernacle of his body, he should be made to pass into the body of a beggar, so as to go about asking alms, and thereafter he shall depart into everlasting punishment. Moreover, as this body pertains to the princes and to matter, it is necessary that he who plants a persea should pass though many bodies until that persea is prostrated. And if one builds a house for himself, he will be divided and scattered among all the bodies. If one bathes in water, he freezes his soul; and if one refuses to give pious regard to his elect, he will be punished through the generations, and will be translated into the

bodies of catechumens, until he render many tributes of piety; and for this reason they offer to the elect whatever is best in their meats. And when they are about to eat bread, they offer up prayer first of all, addressing themselves in these terms to the bread: "I have neither reaped thee, nor ground thee, nor pressed thee, nor cast thee into the baking-vessel; but another has done these things, and brought thee to me, and I have eaten thee without fault." And when he has uttered these things to himself, he says to the catechumen, "I have prayed for thee;" and in this manner that person then takes his departure. For, as I remarked to you a little before, if any one reaps, he will be reaped; and so, too, if one casts grain into the mill, he will be cast in himself in like manner, or if he kneads he will be kneaded, or if he bakes he will be baked; and for this reason they are interdicted from doing any such work. Moreover, there are certain other worlds on which the luminaries rise when they have set on our world. And if a person walks upon the ground here, he injures the earth; and if he moves his hand, he injures the air; for the air is the soul (*life*) of men and living creatures, both fowl, and fish, and creeping thing. And as to everyone existing in this world, I have told you that this body of his does not pertain to God, but to matter, and is itself darkness, and consequently it must needs be cast in darkness.

10. Now, with respect to paradise, it is not called *a cosmos*. The trees that are in it are lust and other seductions, which corrupt the rational powers of those men. And that tree in paradise, by which men know the good, is Jesus Himself, *or* the knowledge of Him in the world. He who partakes thereof discerns the good and the evil. The world itself, however, is not God's *work*; but it

was the structure of a portion of matter, and consequently all things perish in it. And what the princes took as spoil from the first man, that is what makes the moon full, and what is being purged day by day of the world. And if the soul makes its exit without having gained the knowledge of the truth, it is given over to the demons, in order that they may subdue it in the Gehennas of fire; and after that discipline it is made to pass into bodies with the purpose of being brought into subjection, and in this manner it is cast into the mighty fire until the consummation. Again, regarding the prophets amongst you, he speaks thus: Their spirit is one of impiety, or of the lawlessness of the darkness which arose at the beginning. And being deceived by this spirit, they have not spoken *truth*; for the prince blinded their mind. And if anyone follows their words, he dies forever, bound to the clods of earth, because he has not learned the knowledge of the Paraclete. He also gave injunctions to his elect alone, who are not more than seven in number. And the charge was this: "When ye cease eating, pray, and put upon your head an olive, sworn with the invocation of many names for the confirmation of this faith." The names, however, were not made known to me; for only these seven make use of them. And again, the name Sabaoth, which is honorable and mighty with you, he declares to be the nature of man, and the parent of desire; for which reason the simple worship desire, and hold it to be a deity. Furthermore, as regards the manner of the creation of Adam, he tells us that he who said, "Come and let us make man in our image, after our likeness," or "after the form which we have seen," is the prince who addressed the other princes in terms which may be thus interpreted: "Come, give me of the light which we have received, and let us make man after the form of us princes, even after that form which we have seen, that is to say, the first man." And in that manner he created the man. They created Eve also after the like fashion, imparting to her of their own lust, with a view to the deceiving of Adam. And by these means the construction of the world proceeded from the operations of the prince.

11. He holds also that God has no part with the world itself, and finds no pleasure in it, by reason of its having been made a spoil of from the first by the princes, and on account of the ill that rose on it. Wherefore He sends and takes away from them day by day the soul belonging to Him, through the medium of these luminaries, the sun and the moon, by which the whole world and all creation are dominated. Him, again, who spoke with Moses, and the Jews, and the priests, he declares to be the prince of the darkness; so that the Christians, and the Jews, and the Gentiles are one and the same body, worshipping the same God: for He seduces them in His own passions, being no God of truth. For this reason all those who hope in that God who spoke with Moses and the prophets have to be bound together with the said deity, because they have not hoped in the God of truth; for that deity spoke with him in accordance with their own passions. Moreover, after all these things, he speaks in the following terms with regard to the end, as he has also written: When the elder has displayed his image, the Omophorus then lets the earth go from him, and so the mighty fire gets free, and consumes the whole world. Then, again, he lets the soil go with the new æon, in order that all the souls of sinners may be bound for ever. These things will take place at the time when the man's image has come. And all these powers put forth by God,—

namely, Jesus, who is in the smaller ship, and the Mother of Life, and the twelve helmsmen, and the virgin of the light, and the third elder, who is in the greater ship, and the living spirit, and the wall of the mighty fire, and the wall of the wind, and the air, and the water, and the interior living fire,—have their seat in the lesser luminary, until the fire shall have consumed the whole world: and that is to happen within so many years, the exact number of which, however, I have not ascertained. And after these things there will be a restitution of the two natures; and the princes will occupy the lower parts proper to them, and the Father the higher parts, receiving again what is His own due possession.—All this doctrine he delivered to his three disciples, and charged each to journey to a separate clime. The Eastern parts fell thus to the lot of Addas; Thomas obtained the Syrian territories as his heritage; and another, to wit, Hermeias, directed his course towards Egypt. And to this day they, sojourn there, with the purpose of establishing the propositions contained in this doctrine.

12. When Turbo had made this statement, Archelaus was intensely excited; but Marcellus remained unmoved, for he expected that God would come to the help of His truth. Archelaus, however, had additional cares in his anxiety about the people, like the shepherd who becomes concerned for his sheep when secret perils threaten them from the wolves. Accordingly Marcellus loaded Turbo with the most liberal gifts, and instructed him to remain in the house of Archelaus the bishop. But on that selfsame day Manes arrived, bringing along with him certain chosen youths and virgins to the number of twenty-two. And first of all he sought for Turbo at the door of the house of Marcellus; and on failing to find him

there, he went in to salute Marcellus. On seeing him, Marcellus at first was struck with astonishment at the costume in which he presented himself. For he wore a kind of shoe which is usually called in common speech the quadrisole; he had also a party-coloured cloak, of a somewhat airy appearance; in his hand he grasped a very sturdy staff of ebony wood; he carried a Babylonian book under his left arm; his legs were swathed in trousers of different colors, the one being red, and the other green as a leek; and his whole mien was like that of some old Persian master and commandant. Thereupon Marcellus sent forthwith for Archelaus, who arrived so quickly as almost to outstrip the word, and on entering was greatly tempted at once to break out against him, being provoked to that instantly by the very sight of his costume and his appearance, though more especially also by the fact that he had himself been turning over in his mind in his retirement the various matters which he had learned from the recital of Turbo, and had thus come carefully prepared. But Marcellus, in his great thoughtfulness, repressed all zeal for mere wrangling, and decided to hear both parties. With that view he invited the leading men of the city; and from among them he selected as judges *of the discussion* certain adherents of the Gentile religion, four in number. The names of these umpires were as follows: Manippus, a person deeply versed in the art of grammar and the practice of rhetoric; Ægialeus, a very eminent physician, and a man of the highest reputation for learning; and Claudius and Cleobolus, two brothers famed as rhetoricians. A splendid assemblage was thus convened; so large, indeed, that the house of Marcellus, which was of immense size, was filled with those who had been called to be hearers. And when the parties who proposed to speak in opposition to each other had taken their places in view of all, then those who had been elected as judges took their seats in a position elevated above all others: and the task of commencing the disputation was assigned to Manes. Accordingly, when silence was secured, he began the discussion in the following terms:

13. My brethren, I indeed am a disciple of Christ, and, moreover, an apostle of Jesus; and it is owing to the exceeding kindness of Marcellus that I have hastened hither, with the view of showing him clearly in what manner he ought to keep the system of divine religion, so that the said Marcellus verily, who at present has put himself, like one who has surrendered himself prisoner, under the doctrine of Archelaus, may not, like the dumb animals, which are destitute of intellect and understand not what they do, be fatally smitten to the ruin of his soul, in consequence of any failure in the possession of further facilities for setting about the right observance of divine worship. I know, furthermore, and am certain, that if Marcellus is once set right, it will be quite possible that all of you may also have your salvation effected; for your city hangs suspended upon his judgment. If vain presumption is rejected by every one of you, and if those things which are to be declared by me be heard with a real love for the truth, ye will receive the inheritance of the age to come, and the kingdom of heaven. I, in sooth, am the Paraclete, whose mission was announced of old time by Jesus, and who was to come to "convince the world of sin and unrighteousness." And even as Paul, who was sent before me, said of himself, that "he knew in part, and prophesied in part," so I reserve the perfect for myself, in order that I may do away with that which is in part.

Therefore receive ye this third testimony, that I am an elect apostle of Christ; and if ye choose to accept my words, ye will find salvation; but if ye refuse them, eternal fire will have you to consume you. For as Hymenæus and Alexander were "delivered unto Satan, that they might learn not to blaspheme," so will all ye also be delivered unto the prince of punishments, because ye have done injury to the Father of Christ, in so far as ye declare Him to be the cause of all evils, and the founder of unrighteousness, and the creator of all iniquity. By such doctrine ye do, indeed, bring forth from the same fountain both sweet water and bitter,—a thing which can in no possible way be either done or apprehended. For who ought to be believed? Should it be those masters of yours whose enjoyment is in the flesh, and who pamper themselves with the richest delights; or our Savior Jesus Christ, who says, as it is written in the book of the Gospels, "A good tree cannot bring forth evil fruit, neither can a corrupt tree bring forth good fruit," and who in another place assures us that the "father of the devil is a liar and a murderer from the beginning," and tells us again that men's desire was for the darkness, so that they would not follow that Word that had been sent forth in the beginning from the light, and (once more shows us) the man who is the enemy of the same, the sower of tares, and the god and prince of the age of this world, who blinds the minds of men that they may not be obedient to the truth in the Gospel of Christ? Is that God good who has no wish that the men who are his own should be saved? And, not to go over a multitude of other matters, and waste much time, I may defer till another opportunity the exposition of the true doctrine; and taking it for granted that I have said enough on this subject for the present, I may revert to the matter immediately before me, and endeavor satisfactorily to demonstrate the absurdity of these men's teaching, and show that none of these things can be attributed to the God and Father of our Lord and Savior, but that we must take Satan to be the cause of all our ills. To him, certainly, these must be carried back, for all ills of this kind are generated by him. But those things also which are written in the prophets and the law are none the less to be ascribed to him; for he it is who spoke then in the prophets, introducing into their minds very many ignorant notions of God, as well as temptations and passions. They, too, set forth that devourer of blood and flesh; and to that Satan and to his prophets all these things properly pertain which he wished to transfer to the Father of Christ, prepared as he was to write a few things in the way of truth, that by means of these he might also gain credence for those other statements of his which are false. Hence it is well for us to receive nothing at all of all those things which have been written of old even down to John, and indeed to embrace only the kingdom of heaven, which has been preached in the Gospel since his days; for they verily but made a mockery of themselves, introducing as they did things ridiculous and ludicrous, keeping some small words given in obscure outline in the law, but not understanding that, if good things are mixed up with evil, the result is, that by the corruption of these evil things, even those others which are good are destroyed. And if, indeed, there is anyone who may prove himself able to demonstrate that the law upholds the right, that law ought to be kept; but if we can show it to be evil, then it ought to be done away with and rejected, inasmuch as it contains the ministration of death, which was graven, which also covered and destroyed the glory on the countenance of Moses. It is a thing not without peril, therefore, for any one of you to teach the New Testament along with the law and the prophets, as if they were of one and the same origin; for the knowledge of our Savior renews *the one* from day to day, while the other grows old and infirm, and passes almost into utter destruction. And this is a fact manifest to those who are capable of exercising discernment. For just as, when the branches of a tree become aged, or when the trunk ceases to bear fruit any more, they are cut down; and just as, when the members of the body suffer mortification, they are amputated, for the poison of the mortification diffuses itself from these members through the whole body, and unless some remedy be found for the disease by the skill of the physician, the whole body will be vitiated; so, too, if ye receive the law without understanding its origin, ye will ruin your souls, and lose your salvation. For "the law and the prophets were until John;" but since John the law of truth, the law of the promises, the law of heaven, the new law, is made known to the race of man. And, in sooth, as long as there was no one to exhibit to you this most true knowledge of our Lord Jesus, ye had not sin. Now, however, ye both see and hear, and yet ye desire to walk in ignorance, in order that ye may keep that law which has been destroyed and abandoned. And Paul, too, who is held to be the most approved *apostle* with us, expresses himself to the same effect in one of his epistles, when he says: "For if I build again the things which I destroyed, I make myself a prevaricator." And in saying this he pronounces on them as Gentiles, because they were under the elements of the world, before the fulness of faith came, believing then as they did in the law and the prophets.

## The Acts of the Disposition with the Heresiarch Manes

**14.** *The judges said*: If you have any clearer statement yet to make, give us some explanation of the nature of your doctrine and the designation of your faith. *Manes replied*: I hold that there are two natures, one good and another evil; and that the one which is good dwells indeed in certain parts proper to it, but that the evil one is this world, as well as all things in it, which are placed there like objects imprisoned in the portion of the wicked one, as John says, that "the whole world lieth in wickedness," and not in God. Wherefore we have maintained that there are two localities,—one good, and another which lies outside of this, so that, having space therein *in his*, it might be capable of receiving into itself the creature, i.e., *creation*, of the world. For if we say that there is but a monarchy of one nature, and that God fills all things, and that there is no location outside of Him, what will be the sustainer of the creature, i.e., *creation?* where will be the Gehenna of fire? where the outer darkness? where the weeping? Shall I say in Himself? God forbid; else He Himself will also be made to suffer in and with these. Entertain no such fancies, whosoever of you have any care for your salvation; for I shall give you an example, in order that you may have fuller understanding of the truth. The world is one vessel; and if the substance of God has already filled this entire vessel, how is it possible now that anything more can be placed in this same vessel? If it is full, how shall it receive what is placed in it, unless a certain portion of the vessel is emptied? Or whither shall that which is to be emptied out make its way, seeing that there is no locality for it? Where then is the earth? where the heavens? where the abyss? where the stars? where the settlements? where the powers? where the princes? where the outer darkness?

Who is he that has laid the foundations of these, and where? No one is able to tell us that without stumbling on blasphemy. And in what way, again, has He been able to make the creatures, if there is no subsistent matter? For if He has made them out of the non-existent, it will follow that these visible creatures should be superior, and full of all virtues. But if in these there are wickedness, and death, and corruption, and whatever is opposed to the good, how say we that they owe their formation to a nature different from themselves? Howbeit if you consider the way in which the sons of men are begotten, you will find that the creator of man is not the Lord, but another being, who is also himself of an unbegotten nature, who has neither founder, nor creator, nor maker, but who, such as he is, has been produced by his own malice alone. In accordance with this, you men have a commerce with your wives, which comes to you by an occasion of the following nature. When any one of you has satiated himself with carnal meats, and meats of other kinds, then the impulse of concupiscence rises in him, and in this way the enjoyment of begetting a son is increased; and this happens not as if that had its spring in any virtue, or in philosophy, or in any other gift of mind, but in fulness of meats only, and in lust and fornication. And how shall anyone tell me that our father Adam was made after the image of God, and in His likeness, and that he is like Him who made him? How can it be said that all of us who have been begotten of him are like him? Yea, rather, on the contrary, have we not a great variety of forms, and do we not bear the impress of different countenances? And how true this is, I shall exhibit to you in parables. Look, for instance, at a person who wishes to seal up a treasure, or some other object, and you will observe how, when he has got a little wax or clay, he seeks to stamp it with an impression of his own countenance from the ring which he wears; but if another countenance also stamps the figure of itself on the object in a similar manner, will the impression seem like? By no means, although you may be reluctant to acknowledge what is true. But if we are not like in the common impression, and if, instead of that, there are differences in us, how can it fail to be proved thereby that we are the workmanship of the princes, and of matter? For in due accordance with their form, and likeness, and image, we also exist as diverse forms. But if you wish to be fully instructed as to that commerce which took place at the beginning, and as to the manner in which it occurred, I shall explain the matter to you.

15. *The judges said*: We need not inquire as to the manner in which that primitive commerce took place until we have first seen it proved that there are two natural principles. For when once it is made clear that there are two unbegotten natures, then others of your averments may also gain our assent, even although something in them may not seem to fit in very readily with what is credible. For as the power of pronouncing judgment has been committed to us, we shall declare what may make itself clear to our mind. We may, however, also grant to Archelaus the liberty of speaking to these statements of yours, so that, by comparing what is said by each of you, we may be able to give our decision in accordance with the truth. *Archelaus said*: Notwithstanding, the adversary's intent is replete with gross audacity and blasphemy. *Manes said*: Hear, O judges, what he has said *of the adversary*. He admits, then, that there are two objects. *Archelaus said*: It seems to me that this man is full of madness rather than of prudence, who would stir

up a controversy with me to-day because I chance to speak of the *adversary*. But this objection of yours may be removed with few words, notwithstanding that you have supposed from this expression of mine that I shall allow that there are these two natures. You have come forward with a most extravagant doctrine; for neither of the assertions made by you holds good. For it is quite possible that one who is an adversary, not by nature, but by determination, may be made a friend, and cease to be an adversary; and thus, when the one of us has come to acquiesce with the other, we twain shall appear to be, as it were, one and the same object. This account also indicates that rational creatures have been entrusted with free-will, in virtue of which they also admit of conversions. And consequently there cannot be *two* unbegotten natures. What do you say, then? Are these two natures inconvertible? or are they convertible? or is one of them converted? *Manes*, however, held back, because he did not find a suitable reply; for he was pondering the conclusion which might be drawn from either of two answers which he might make, turning the matter over thus in his thoughts: If I say that they are converted, he will meet me with that statement which is recorded in the Gospel about the trees; but if I say that they are not convertible, he will necessarily ask me to explain the condition and cause of their intermingling. In the meantime, after a little delay, *Manes replied:* They are indeed both inconvertible in so far as contraries are concerned; but they are convertible as far as properties are concerned. *Archelaus then said:* You seem to me to be out of your mind, and oblivious of your own propositions; yea, you do not appear even to recognize the powers or qualities of the very words which you have been learning.

For you do not understand either what conversion is, or what is meant by *unbegotten*, or what duality implies, or what is past, or what is present, or what is future, as I have gathered from the opinions to which you have just now given expression. For you have affirmed, indeed, that each of these two natures is inconvertible so far as regards contraries, but convertible so far as regards properties. But I maintain that one who moves in properties does not pass out of himself, but subsists in these same properties, in which he is ever inconvertible; while in the case of one who is susceptible of conversion, the effect is that he is placed outside the pale of properties, and passes within the sphere of accidents.

16. *The judges said:* Convertibility translates the person whom it befalls into another; as, for example, we might say that if a Jew were to make up his mind to become a Christian, or, on the other hand, if a Christian were to decide to be a Gentile, this would be a species of convertibility, and a cause of the same. But, again, if we suppose a Gentile to keep by all his own *heathen* properties, and to offer sacrifices to his gods, and to do service to the temples as usual, surely you would not be of opinion that he could be said to be converted, while he yet holds by his properties, and goes on in them? What, then, do you say? Do they sustain convertibility or not? *And as Manes hesitated, Archelaus proceeded thus*: If, indeed, he says that both natures are convertible, what is there to prevent our thinking them to be one and the same object? For if they are inconvertible, then surely in natures which are similarly inconvertible and similarly unbegotten there is no distinction, neither can the one of them be recognized as good or as evil. But if they are both convertible, then, forsooth, the possible result may be

both that the good is made evil, and that the evil is made good. If, however, this is the possible result, why should we not speak of one only as unbegotten, which would be a conception in worthier accordance with the reckoning of truth? For we have to consider how that evil one became so at first, or against what objects he exercised his wickedness before the formation of the world. When the heavens had not yet appeared, when the earth did not yet subsist, and when there was neither man nor animal, against whom did he put his wickedness in operation? whom did he oppress unjustly? whom did he rob and kill? But if you say that he first appeared in his evil nature to his own kin, then without doubt you give the proof that he comes of a good nature. And if, again, all these are also evil, how can Satan then cast out Satan? But while thus reduced to a dilemma on this point, you may change your position in the discussion, and say that the good suffered violence from the evil. But none the more is it without peril for you to make such a statement, to the effect of affirming the vanquishing of the light; for what is vanquished has destruction near it. For what says the divine word? "Who can enter into a strong man's house, and spoil his goods, except he be stronger than he?" But if you allege that he first appeared in his evil nature to men, and only from that time showed openly the marks of his wickedness, then it follows that before this time he was good, and that he took on this quality of conversion because the creation of man was found to have emerged as the cause of his wickedness. But, in fine, let him tell us what he understands by evil, lest perchance he may be defending or setting up a mere name. And if it is not the name but the substance of evil that he speaks of, then let him set before us the fruits of this wickedness and iniquity, since the nature of a tree can never be known but by its fruit.

17. *Manes said*: Let it first be allowed on your side that there is an alien root of wickedness, which God has not planted, and then I shall tell you its fruits. *Archelaus said:* Truth's reckoning does not make any such requirement; and I shall not admit to you that there is a root of any such evil tree, of the fruit whereof no one has ever tasted. But just as, when a man desires to make any purchase, he does not produce the money unless he first ascertains by tasting the object whether it is of a dry or a moist species, so I shall not admit to you that the tree is evil and utterly corrupt, unless the quality of its fruit is first exhibited; for it is written, that "the tree is known by its fruits." Tell us, therefore, O Manes, what fruit is yielded by that tree which is called evil, or of what nature it is, and what virtue it is, that we may also believe with you that the root of that same tree is of that character which you ascribe to it. *Manes said:* The root indeed is evil, and the tree is most corrupt, but the increase is not from God. Moreover, fornications, adulteries, murders, avarice, and all evil deeds, are the fruits of that evil root. *Archelaus said:* That we may credit you when you say that these are the fruits of that evil root, give us a taste of these things; for you have pronounced the substance of this tree to be ungenerate, the fruits of which are produced after its own likeness. *Manes said:* The very unrighteousness which subsists in men offers the proof itself, and in avarice too you may taste that evil root. *Archelaus said:* Well, then, as you have stated the question, those iniquities which prevail among men are fruits of this tree. *Manes said:* Quite so. *Archelaus proceeded:* If these, then, are the fruits, that is to say, the

wicked deeds of men, it will follow that the men themselves will hold the place of the root and of the tree; for you have declared that they produce fruits of this nature. *Manes said:* That is my statement. *Archelaus answered:* Not well say you, *That is my statement*: for surely that cannot be your statement; otherwise, when men cease from sinning, this tree of wickedness will appear to be unfruitful. *Manes said:* What you say is an impossibility; for even though one or another, or several, were to cease sinning, there would yet be others doing evil still. *Archelaus said:* If it is at all possible for one or another, or several, as you admit, not to sin, it is also possible for all to do the same; for they are all of one parent, and are all men of one lump. And, not to follow at my ease those affirmations which you have so confusedly made through all their absurdities, I shall conclude their refutation by certain unmistakeable counter-arguments. Do you allege that the fruits of the evil root and the evil tree are the deeds of men, that is to say, fornications, adulteries, perjuries, murders, and other similar things? *Manes said:* I do. *Archelaus said:* Well, then, if it happened that the race of men was to die off the face of the earth, so that they should not be able to sin anymore, the substance of that tree would then perish, and it would bear fruit no more. *Manes said:* And when will that take place of which you speak? *Archelaus said:* What is in the future I know not, for I am but a man; nevertheless I shall not leave these words of yours unexamined. What say you of the race of men? Is it unbegotten, or is it a production? *Manes said:* It is a production. *Archelaus said:* If man is a production, who is the parent of adultery and fornication, and such other things? Whose fruit is this? Before man was made, who was there to be a fornicator, or an adulterer, or a murderer? *Manes said:* But if the man is fashioned of the evil nature, it is manifest that he is such a fruit, albeit he may sin, albeit he may not sin; whence also the name and race of men are once for all and absolutely of this character, whether they may do what is righteous or what is unrighteous. *Archelaus said:* Well, we may also take notice of that matter. If, as you aver, the wicked one himself made man, why is it that he practices his malignity on him?

18. *The judges said:* We desire to have information from you on this point, Manichæus, to wit, to what effect you have affirmed him to be evil. Do you mean that he has been so from the time when men were made, or before that period? For it is necessary that you should give some proof of his wickedness from the very time from which you declare him to have been evil. Be assured that the quality of a wine cannot be ascertained unless one first tastes it; and understand that, in like manner, every tree is known by its fruit. What say you, then? From what time has this personality been evil? For an explanation of this problem seems to us to be necessary. *Manes said:* He has always been so. *Archelaus said:* Well, then, I shall also show from this, most excellent friends, and most judicious auditors, that his statement is by no means correct. For iron, to take an example, has not been an evil thing always, but only from the period of man's existence, and since his art turned it to evil by applying it to false uses; and every sin has come into existence since the period of man's being. Even that great serpent himself was not evil previous to man, but only after man, in whom he displayed the fruit of his wickedness, because he willed it himself. If, then, the father of wickedness makes his appearance to us after

man *has come into being*, according to the Scriptures, how can he be unbegotten who has thus been constituted evil subsequently to man, who is himself a production? But, again, why should he exhibit himself as evil just from the period when, on your supposition, he did himself create man? What did he desire in him? If man's whole body was his own workmanship, what did he ardently affect in him? For one who ardently affects or desires, desires something which is different and better. If, indeed, man takes his origin from him in respect of the evil nature, we see how man was his own, as I have frequently shown. For if man was his own, he was also evil himself, just as it holds with our illustration of the like tree and the like fruit; for an evil tree, as you say, produces evil fruit. And seeing that all were evil, what did he desiderate, or in what could he show the beginning of his wickedness, if from the time of man's formation man was the cause of his wickedness? Moreover, the law and precept having been given to the man himself, the man had not by any means the power to yield obedience to the serpent, and to the statements which were made by him; and had the man then yielded no obedience to him, what occasion would there have been for him to be evil? But, again, if evil is unbegotten, how does it happen that man is sometimes found to be stronger than it? For, by obeying the law of God, he will often overcome every root of wickedness; and it would be a ridiculous thing if he, who is but the production, should be found to be stronger than the unbegotten. Moreover, whose is that law with its commandment—that commandment, I mean, which has been given to man? Without doubt it will be acknowledged to be God's. And how, then, can the law be given to an alien? or who can give his commandment to an enemy? Or, to speak of him who receives the commandment, how can he contend against the devil? that is to say, on this supposition, how can he contend against his own creator, as if the son, while he is a debtor to him for deeds of kindness, were to choose to inflict injuries on the father? Thus you but mark out the profitlessness of man on this side, if you suppose him to be contradicting by the law and commandment him who has made him, and to be making the effort to get the better of him. Yea, we shall have to fancy the devil himself to have gone to such an excess of folly, as not to have perceived that in making man he made an adversary for himself, and neither to have considered what might be his future, nor to have foreseen the actual consequence of his act; whereas even in ourselves. who are but productions, there are at least some small gifts of knowledge, and a measure of prudence, and a moderate degree of consideration, which is sometimes of a very trustworthy nature. And how, then, can we believe that in the unbegotten there is not some little portion of prudence, or consideration, or intelligence? Or how can we make the contrary supposition, according to your assertion, namely, that he is discovered to be of the most senseless apprehension, and the dullest heart and in short rather like the brutes in his natural constitution? But if the case stands thus, again, how is it that man, who is possessed of no insignificant power in mental capacity and knowledge, could have received his substance from one who thus is, of all beings, the most ignorant and the bluntest in apprehension? How shall anyone be rash enough to profess that man is the workmanship of an author of this character? But, again, if man consists both of soul and of body, and not merely of body without soul, and if the one cannot subsist apart from the other, why will you assert that these two are antagonistic and contrary to each other? For our Lord Jesus Christ, indeed, seems to me to have spoken of these in His parables, when He said: "No man can put new wine into old bottles, else the bottles will break, and the wine run out." But new wine is to be put into new bottles, as there is indeed one and the same Lord for the bottle and for the wine. For although the substance may be different, yet by these two substances, in their due powers, and in the maintenance of their proper mutual relations, the one person of man subsists. We do not say, indeed, that the soul is of one substance with the body, but we aver that they have each their own characteristic qualities; and as the bottle and the wine are applied in the similitude to one race and one species of men, so truth's reckoning requires us to grant that man was produced complete by the one God: for the soul rejoices in the body, and loves and cherishes it; and none the less does the body rejoice that it is quickened by the soul. But if, on the other hand, a person maintains that the body is the work of the wicked one, inasmuch as it is so corruptible, and antiquated, and worthless, it would follow then that it is incapable of sustaining the virtue of the spirit or the movement of the soul, and the most splendid creation of the same. For just as, when a person puts a piece of new cloth into an old garment, the rent is made worse; so also the body would perish if it were to be associated, under such conditions, with that most brilliant production the soul. Or, to use another illustration: just as, when a man carries the light of a lamp into a dark place the darkness is forthwith put to flight and makes no appearance; so we ought to understand that, on the soul's introduction into the body the darkness is straightway banished, and one nature at once effected, and one man constituted in one species. And thus, agreeably therewith, it will be allowed that the new wine is put into new bottles, and that the piece of new cloth is not put into the old garment. But from this we are able to show that there is a unison of powers in these two substances, that is to say, in that of the body and in that of the soul; of which unison that greatest teacher in the Scriptures, Paul, speaks, when he tells us, that "God hath set the members every one of them in the body as it hath pleased Him."

19. But if it seems difficult for you to understand this, and if you do not acquiesce in these statements, I may at all events try to make them good by adducing illustrations. Contemplate man as a kind of temple, according to the similitude of Scripture: the spirit that is in man may thus be likened to the image that dwells in the temple. Well, then, a temple cannot be constituted unless first an occupant is acknowledged for the temple; and, on the other hand, an occupant cannot be settled in the temple unless the structure has been erected. Now, since these two objects, the occupant and the structure, are both consecrated together, how can any antagonism or contrariety be found between them, and how should it not rather appear that they have both been the products of subjects that are in amity and of one mind? And that you may know that this is the case, and that these subjects are truly at one both in fellowship and in lineage, He who knows and hears *all* has made this response, "Let us make man," and so forth. For he who constructs the temple interrogates him who fashions the image, and inquires carefully about the measurements of magnitude, and breadth, and bulk, in order that he may mark off the space for the foundations in accordance with these dimensions;

and no one sets about the vain task of building a temple without first making himself acquainted with the measurement needed for the placing of the image. In like manner, therefore, the mode and the measure of the body are made the subject of inquiry, in order that the soul may be appropriately lodged in it by God, the Artificer of all things. But if anyone say that he who has molded the body is an enemy to the God who is the Creator of my soul, then how is it that, while regarding each other with a hostile eye, these two parties have not brought disrepute upon the work, by bringing it about either that he who constructs the temple should make it of such narrow dimensions as to render it incapable of accommodating what is placed within it, or that he who fashions the image should come with something so massive and ponderous, that, on its introduction into the temple, the edifice would at once collapse? If such is not the case, then, with these things, let us contemplate them in the light of what we know to be the objects and intents of antagonists. But if it is right for all to be disposed with the same measures and the same equity, and to be displayed with like glory, what doubt should we still entertain on this subject? We add, if it please you, this one illustration more. Man appears to resemble a ship which has been constructed by the builder and launched into the deep, which, however, it is impossible to navigate without the rudder, by which it can be kept under command, and turned in whatsoever direction its steersman may wish to sail. Also, that the rudder and the whole body of the ship require the same artificer, is a matter admitting no doubt; for without the rudder the whole structure of the ship, that huge body, will be an inert mass. And thus, then, we say that the soul is the rudder of the body; that both these, moreover, are

## The Acts of the Disposition with the Heresiarch Manes

ruled by that liberty of judgment and sentiment which we possess, and which corresponds to the steersman; and that when these two are made one by union, and thus possess a unison of function applicable to all kinds of work, whatever may be the products of their own operation, they bear a testimony to the fact that they have both one and the same author and maker.

20. On hearing these argumentations, the multitudes who were present were exceedingly delighted; so much so, indeed, that they were almost laying hands on Manes; and it was with difficulty that Archelaus restrained them, and kept them back, and made them quiet again. *The judges said:* Archelaus has given us proof sufficient of the fact that the body and soul of man are the works of one hand; because an object cannot subsist in any proper consonance and unison as the work of one hand, if there is any want of harmony in the design and plan. But if it is alleged that one could not possibly have sufficed to develop both these objects, *namely, body and soul*, this is simply to exhibit the incapacity of the artificer. For thus, even though one should grant that the soul is the creation of a good deity, it will be found to be but an idle work so far as the man is concerned, unless it also takes to itself the body. And if, again, the body is held to be the formation of an evil deity, the work will also none the less be idle unless it receives the soul; and, in truth, unless the soul be in unison with the body by commixture and due introduction, so that the two are in mutual connections, the man will not exist, neither can we speak of him. Hence *we are of opinion that* Archelaus has proved by a variety of illustrations that there is but one and the same maker for the whole man. *Archelaus said:* I doubt not, Manes, that you understand this, namely, that

one who is born and created is called the son of him who begets or creates. But if the wicked one made man, then he ought to be his father, according to nature. And to whom, then, did the Lord Jesus address Himself, when in these terms He taught men to pray: "When ye pray, say, Our Father which art in heaven;" and again, "Pray to your Father which is in secret?" But it was of Satan that He spoke when He said, that He "beheld him as lightning fall from heaven;" so that no one dare say that He taught us to pray to him. And surely Jesus did not come down from heaven with the purpose of bringing men together, and reconciling them to Satan; but, on the contrary, He gave him over to be bruised beneath the feet of His faithful ones. However, for my part, I would say that those Gentiles are the more blessed who do indeed bring in a multitude of deities, but at least hold them all to be of one mind, and in amity with each other; whereas this man, though he brings in but two gods, does not blush to posit enmities and discordant sentiments between them. And, in sooth, if these *Gentiles* were to bring in their counterfeit deities under conditions of that kind, we would verily have it in our power to witness something like a gladiatorial contest proceeding between them, with their innumerable natures and diverse sentiments.

21. But now, what it is necessary for me to say on the subject of the inner and the outer man, may be expressed in the words of the Savior to those who swallow a camel, and wear the outward garb of the hypocrite, begirt with blandishments and flatteries. It is to them that Jesus addresses Himself when He says: "Woe unto you, scribes and Pharisees, hypocrites! for ye make clean the outside of the cup and of the platter, but within they are full of uncleanness. Or know you not, that He

that made that which is without, made that which is within also?" Now why did He speak of the cup and of the platter? Was He who uttered these words a glassworker, or a potter who made vessels of clay? Did He not speak most manifestly of the body and the soul? For the Pharisees truly looked to the "tithing of anise and cummin, and left undone the weightier matters of the law;" and while devoting great care to the things which were external, they overlooked those which bore upon the salvation of the soul. For they also had respect to "greetings in the market-place," and "to the uppermost seats at feasts:" and to them the Lord Jesus, knowing their perdition, made this declaration, that they attended to those things only which were without, and despised as strange things those which were within, and understood not that He who made the body made also the soul. And who is so unimpressible and stolid in intellect, as not to see that those sayings *of our Lord* may suffice him for all cases? Moreover, it is in perfect harmony with these sayings that Paul speaks, when he interprets to the following intent certain things written in the law: "Thou shalt not muzzle the mouth of the ox that treaded out the corn. Doth God take care for oxen? Or saith He it altogether for our sakes?" But why should we waste further time upon this subject? Nevertheless I shall add a few things out of many that might be offered. Suppose now that there are two unbegotten *principles*, and that we determine fixed localities for these: it follows then that God is separated, if He is *supposed to be* within a certain location, and not diffused everywhere; and He will consequently *be represented as* much inferior to the locality in which He is understood to be *for the object which contains is always greater than the object which is contained in it:* and thus God is made to be of that magnitude which corresponds with the magnitude of the locality in which He is contained, just as is the case with a man in a house. Then, further, reason asks who it is that has divided between them, or who has appointed for them their determinate limits; and thus both would be made out to be the decided inferiors of man's own power. For Lysimachus and Alexander held the empire of the whole world, and were able to subdue all foreign nations, and the whole race of men; so that throughout that period there was no other in possession of empire besides themselves under heaven. And how will anyone be rash enough to say that God, who is the true light that never suffers eclipse, and whose is also the kingdom that is holy and everlasting, is not everywhere present, as is the way with this most depraved man, who, in his impiety, refuses to ascribe to the Omnipotent God even equal power with men?

22. *The judges said:* We know that a light shines through the whole house, and not in some single part of it; as Jesus also intimates when He says, that "no man lighting a candle puts it under a bushel, but on a candlestick, that it may give light unto all that are in the house." If, then, God is a light, it must needs be that light (if Jesus is to be credited) shall shine on the whole world, and not on any portions of it merely. And if, then, that light holds possession of the whole world, where now can there be any ungenerated darkness? or how can darkness be understood to exist at all, unless it is something simply accidental? *Archelaus said:* Forasmuch, indeed, as the word of the Gospel is understood much better by you than by this person who puts himself forward as the Paraclete, although I could call him rather parasite than paraclete, I

shall tell you how it has happened that there is darkness. When the light had been diffused everywhere, God began to constitute the universe, and commenced with the heaven and the earth; in which process this issue appeared, to wit, that the midst, which is the locality of earth covered with shadow, as a consequence of the interposition of the creatures which were called into being, was found to be obscure, in such wise that circumstances required light to be introduced into that place, which was thus situated in the midst. Hence in Genesis, where Moses gives an account of the construction of the world, he makes no mention of the darkness either as made or as not made. But he keeps silent on that subject, and leaves the explanation of it to be discovered by those who may be able to give proper attention to it. Neither, indeed, is that a very arduous and difficult task. For to whom may it not be made plain that this sun of ours is visible, when it has risen in the east, and taken its course toward the west, but that when it has gone beneath the earth, and been carried farther within that formation which among the Greeks is called the *sphere*, it then ceases to appear, being overshadowed in darkness in consequence of the interposition of the bodies? When it is thus covered, and when the body of the earth stands opposite it, a shadow is superinduced, which produces from itself the darkness; and it continues so until again, after the course of the inferior space has been traversed in the night, it rolls towards the east, and is seen to rise once more in its wonted seats. Thus, then, the cause of the shadow and the night is discovered in the solidity of the body of the earth,—a thing, indeed, which a man may understand from the fact of the shadow cast by his own body. For before the heaven and the earth and all those corporeal creatures appeared, the light remained always constant, without waning or eclipse, as there existed no body which might produce shadow by its opposition or intervention; and consequently one must say that nowhere was there darkness then, and nowhere night. For if, to take an illustration, it should please Him who has the power of all things to do away with the quarter which lies to the west, then, as the sun would not direct its course toward that region, there would nowhere emerge either evening or darkness, but the sun would be on its course always, and would never set, but would almost always hold the center tract of heaven, and would never cease to appear; and by this the whole world would be illumined with the clearest light, in virtue of which no part of it would suffer obscuration, but the equal power of one light would remain everywhere. But on the other hand, while the western quarter keeps its position, and the sun executes its course in three parts of the world, then those who are under the sun will be seen to be illuminated more brightly; so that I might almost say, that while the people who belong to the diverse tract are still asleep, those former are in possession of the day's beginning. But just as those Orientals have the light rising on them earlier than the people who live in the west, so they have it also more quickly obscured, and they only who are settled in the middle of the globe see always an equality of light. For when the sun occupies the middle of the heavens, there is no place that can appear to be either brighter or darker (than another), but all parts of the world are illuminated equally and impartially by the sun's effulgence. If, then, as we have said above, that portion of the western tract were done away with, the part which is adjacent to it would now no more suffer obscuration. And these things I could indeed set forth somewhat more simply, as I might also describe the zodiacal circle; but I have not thought of looking into these matters at present. I shall therefore say nothing of these, but shall revert to that capital objection urged by my adversary, in his affirming so strenuously that the darkness is ungenerated; which position, however, has also been confuted already, as far as that could have been done by us.

23. *The judges said:* If we consider that the light existed before the estate of the creatures was introduced, and that there was no object in an opposite position which might generate shadow, it must follow that the light was then diffused everywhere, and that all places were illuminated with its effulgence, as has been shown by what you have stated just now; and as we perceive that the true explanation is given in that, we assign the palm to the affirmations of Archelaus. For if the universe is clearly divided, as if some wall had been drawn through the center of it, and if on the one side the light dwells, and on the other side the darkness, it is yet to be understood that this darkness has been brought accidentally about through the shadow generated in consequence of the objects which have been set up in the world; and hence again we must ask who it is that has built this wall between the two divisions, provided you indeed admit the existence of such a construction, O Manichæus. But if we have to take account of this matter on the supposition that no such wall has been built, then again it comes to be understood that the universe forms but one locality, without any exception, and is placed under one power; and if so, then the darkness can in no way have an ungenerated nature. *Archelaus said:* Let him also explain the following subject with a view to what has been

propounded. If God is seated in His kingdom, and if the wicked one in like manner is seated in his kingdom, who can have constructed the wall between them? For no object can divide two substances except one that is greater than either, even as it is said in the book of Genesis, that "God divided the light from the darkness." Consequently the constructor of this wall must also be some one of a capacity like that: for the wall marks the boundaries of these two parties, just as among people who dwell in the rural parts a stone is usually taken to mark off the portion of each several party; which custom, however, would afford a better apprehension of the case were we to take the division to refer especially to the marking out of an inheritance falling to brothers. But for the present I have not to speak of matters like these, however essential they may appear. For what we are in quest of is an answer to the question, Who can have constructed the wall required for the designation of the limits of the kingdom of each of these twain? No answer has been given. Let not this perfidious fellow hesitate, but let him now acknowledge that the substance of his duality has been reduced again to a unity. Let him mention any one who can have constructed that middle wall. What could the one of these two parties have been engaged in when the other was building? Was he asleep? or was he ignorant of the fact? or was he unable to withstand the attempt? or was he bought over with a price? Tell us what he was about, or tell us who in all the universe was the person that raised the construction. I address my appeal to you, O judges, whom God has sent to us with the fullest plenitude of intelligence; judge ye which of these two could have erected the structure, or what the one could have been doing all the while that the other was engaged in the building.

24. *The judges said:* Tell us, O Manes, who designated the boundaries for the kingdom of each, and who made the middle wall? For Archelaus begs that due importance be attached to the practice of interrogation in this discussion. *Manes said:* The God who is good, and who has nothing in common with evil, placed the firmament in the midst, in order to make it plain that the wicked one is an alien to Him. *Archelaus said:* How fearfully you belie the dignity of that name! You do indeed call Him God, but you do so in name only, and you make His deity resemble man's infirmities. At one time out of the non-existent, and at another time out of underlying matter, which indeed thus existed before Himself, you assert that He did build the structure, as builders among men are wont to do. Sometimes also you speak of Him as apprehensive, and sometimes as variable. It is, however, the part of God to do what is proper to God, and it is the part of man to do what is proper to man. If, then, God, as you say, has constructed a wall, this is a God who marks Himself out as apprehensive, and as possessed of no fortitude. For we know that it is always the case that those who are suspicious of the preparation of secret perils against them by strangers, and who are afraid of the plots of enemies, are accustomed to surround their cities with walls, by which procedure they at once secure themselves in their ignorance, and display their feeble capacity. But here, too, we have something which ought not to be passed over by us in silence, but rather brought prominently forward; so that even by the great abundance of our declarations on the subject our adversary's manifold craftiness may be brought to nought,

with the help of the truth on our side. We may grant, then, that the structure of the wall has been made with the purpose of serving to distinguish between the two kingdoms; for without this one division it is impossible for either of them to have his own proper kingdom. But granting this, then it follows further that in the same manner it will also be impossible for the wicked one to pass without his own proper limits and invade the territories of the good *King*, inasmuch as the wall stands there as an obstacle, unless it should chance first to be cast down, for we have heard that such things have been done by enemies, and indeed with our own eyes we have quite recently seen an achievement of that nature successfully carried out. And when a king attacks a citadel surrounded by a strong wall, he uses first of all the ballista and projectiles; then he endeavors to cut through the gates with axes, and to demolish the walls by the battering-rams; and when he at last obtains an entrance, and gains possession of the place, he does whatever he listed, whether it be his pleasure to carry off the citizens into captivity, or to make a complete destruction of the fortress and its contents, or whether, on the other hand, it may be his will to grant indulgence to the captured stronghold on the humble suit of the conquered. What, then, does my opponent here say to this analogy? Did no adversary substantially—which is as much as to say, designedly—overthrow the muniment cast up between the two? For in his former statements he has avouched that the darkness passed without its own limits, and supervened upon the kingdom of the good God. Who, then, overthrew that munition before the one could thus have crossed over to the other? For it was impossible for the evil one to find any entrance while the munition stood fast. Why are you silent? Why do you hesitate, Manichæus? Yet, although you may hold back, I shall proceed with the task of my own accord. For if we suppose you to say that God destroyed it, then I have to ask what moved Him in this way to demolish the very thing which He had Himself previously constructed on account of the importunity of the wicked one, and for the purpose of preserving the separation between them? In what fit of passion, or under what sense of injury, did He thus set about contending against Himself? Or was it that He lusted after some of the possessions of the wicked one? But if none of these things formed the real cause that led God to destroy those very things which He had constructed a long time before with the view of estranging and separating the wicked one from Him, then it must needs be considered no matter of surprise if God should also have become delighted with his society; for, on your supposition, the munition which had been set up with the purpose of securing God against trouble from him, will appear to have been removed just because now he is to be regarded no more as an enemy, but as a friend. And, on the other hand, if you aver that the wall was destroyed by the wicked one, tell us then how it can be possible for the works of the good God to be mastered by the wicked one. For if that is possible, then the evil nature will be proved to be stronger than God. Furthermore, how can that being, seeing that he is pure and total darkness, surprise the light and apprehend it, while the evangelist gives us the testimony that "the light shineth in darkness, and the darkness comprehended it not?" How is this blind one armed? How does the darkness fight against the kingdom of light? For even as the creatures of God here cannot take in the rays of the sun with uninjured eye, so neither can that being bear the clear vision of the kingdom of light, but he remains forever a stranger to it, and an alien.

25. *Manes said:* Not all receive the word of God, but only those to whom it is given to know the mysteries of the kingdom of heaven. And even now I know who are ours; for "my sheep," He says, "hear my voice." For the sake of those who belong to us, and to whom is given the understanding of the truth, I shall speak in similitudes. The wicked one is like a lion that sought to steal upon the flock of the good shepherd; and when the shepherd saw this, he dug a huge pit, and took one kid out of the flock and cast it into the pit. Then the lion, hungering to get at it, and bursting with passion to devour it, ran up to the pit and fell in, and discovered no strength sufficient to bring him out again. And thereupon the shepherd seized him and shut him up carefully in a den, and at the same time secured the safety of the kid which had been with him in the pit. And it is in this way that the wicked one has been enfeebled,—the lion, so to speak, possessing no more capacity for doing aught injurious; and so all the race of souls will be saved, and what once perished will yet be restored to its proper flock. *Archelaus said*: If you compare the wicked one to the lion, and God to the true shepherd, tell us, whereunto shall we liken the sheep and the kid? *Manes said*: The sheep and the kid seem to me to be of one nature: and they are taken as figures of souls. *Archelaus said*: Well, then, God gave a soul over to perdition when He set it before the lion in the pit. *Manes said*: By no means; far from it. But He was moved by a particular disposition, and in the future He will save that other, *the soul. Archelaus said*: Now, surely it would be an absurd procedure, my hearers, if a shepherd who dreaded the inroad of a lion were to expose to the beast's

devouring fury a lamb that he was wont to carry in his bosom, and if it were then to be said that he meant to save the creature hereafter. Is not this something supremely ridiculous? Yea, there is no kind of sense in this. For *on the supposition implied in your similitude* God thus handed over to Satan a soul that he might seize and ruin. But when did the shepherd ever do anything like that? Did not David deliver a sheep out of the mouth of a lion or of a bear? And we mention this on account of the expression, *out of the mouth of the lion*; for, on your theory, this would imply that the shepherd can bring forth out of the mouth of the lion, or out of the belly of the same, the very object which it has devoured. But you will perhaps make this answer, that it is of God we speak, and that He is able to do all things. Hear, however, what I have to say to that: Why then do you not rather assert His real capacity, and affirm simply His ability to overcome the lion in His own might, or with the pure power of God, and without the help of any sort of cunning devices, or by consigning a kid or a lamb to a pit? Tell me this, too, if the lion were to be supposed to come upon the shepherd at a time when he has no sheep, what would the consequence be? For he who is here called the shepherd is supposed to be unbegotten, and he who is here the lion is also unbegotten. Wherefore, when man did not yet exist—in other words, before the shepherd had a flock—if the lion had then come upon the shepherd, what would have followed, seeing that there could have been nothing for the lion to eat before the kid was in existence? *Manes said*: The lion certainly had nothing to devour, but yet he exercised his wickedness on whatever he was able to light upon as he coursed over the peaks of the mountains; and if at any time food was a matter of necessity with him, he seized some of the beasts which were under his own kingdom. *Archelaus said*: Are these two objects, then, of one substance—the beasts which are under the kingdom of the wicked one, and the kids which are in the kingdom of the good God? *Manes said*: Far from it; not at all: they have nothing in common either between themselves or between the properties which pertain to them severally. *Archelaus said:* There is but one and the same use made of the food in the lion's eating. And though he sometimes got that food from the beasts belonging to himself, and sometimes from those belonging to the good God, there is still no difference between them as far as regards the meats furnished; and from this it is apparent that those are of but one substance. On the other hand, if we say that there is a great difference between the two, we do but ascribe ignorance to the shepherd, in so far as he did not present or set before the lion food adapted to his use, but rather alien meats. Or perchance again, in your desire to dissemble your real position, you will say to me that lion ate nothing. Well, supposing that to be the case, did God then in this way challenge that being to devour a soul while he knew not how to devour aught? and was the pit not the only thing which God sought to employ with the view of cheating him?—if indeed it is at all worthy of God to do that sort of thing, or to contrive deceitful schemes. And that would be to act like a king who, when war is made upon him, puts no kind of confidence in his own strength, but gets paralyzed with the fears of his own feebleness, and shuts himself up within the walls of his city, and erects around him a rampart and other fortifications, and gets them all equipped, and trusts nothing to his own hand and prowess; whereas, if he is a brave man, the king so placed will march a great distance from his own territories to meet the enemy there, and will put forth every possible exertion until he conquers and brings his adversary into his power.

26. *The judges said*: If you allege that the shepherd exposed the kid or the lamb to the lion, when the said lion was meditating an assault on the unbegotten, the case is closed. For seeing that the shepherd of the kids and lambs is himself proved to be in fault to them, on what creature can he pronounce judgment, if it happens that the lamb which has been given up through the shepherd's weakness has proved unable to withstand the lion, and if the consequence is that the lamb has had to do whatever has been the lion's pleasure? Or, to take another instance, that would be just as if a master were to drive out of his house, or deliver over in terror to his adversary, one of his slaves, whom he is unable afterwards to recover by his own strength. Or supposing that by any chance it were to come about that the slave was recovered, on what reasonable ground could the master inflict the torture on him, if it should turn out that the man yielded obedience to all that the enemy laid upon him, seeing that it was the master himself who gave him up to the enemy, just as the kid was given up to the lion? You affirm, too, that the shepherd understood the whole case beforehand. Surely, then, the lamb, when under the lash, and interrogated by the shepherd as to the reason why it had submitted to the lion in these matters, would make some such answer as this: "Thou didst thyself deliver me over to the lion, and thou didst offer no resistance to him, although thou didst know and foresee what would be my lot, when it was necessary for me to yield myself to his commandments." And, not to dilate on this at greater length, we may say that *by such an illustration* neither is God exhibited as a

perfect shepherd, nor is the lion shown to have tasted alien meats; and consequently, under the instruction of the truth itself, it has been made clear that we ought to give the palm to the reasonings adduced by Archelaus. *Archelaus said*: Considering that, on all the points which we have hitherto discussed, the thoughtfulness of the judges has assigned us the amplest scope, it will be well for us to pass over other subjects in silence, and reserve them for another period. For just as, if a person once crushes the head of a serpent, he will not need to lop off any of the other members of its body; so, if we once dispose of this question of the duality, as we have endeavored to do to the best of our ability, other matters which have been maintained in connection with it may be held to be exploded along with it. Nevertheless, I shall yet address myself, at least in a few sentences, to the assertor of these opinions himself, who is now in our presence; so that it may be thoroughly understood by all who he is, and whence he comes, and what manner of person he proves himself to be. For he has given out that he is that Paraclete whom Jesus on His departure promised to send to the race of man for the salvation of the souls of the faithful; and this profession he makes as if he were somewhat superior even to Paul, who was an elect vessel and a called apostle, and who on that ground, while preaching the true doctrine, said: "Or seek ye a proof of that Christ who speaks in me?" What I have to say, however, may become clearer by such an illustration as the following:—A certain man gathered into his store a very large quantity of corn, so that the place was perfectly full. This place he shut and sealed in a thoroughly satisfactory fashion, and gave directions to keep careful watch over it. And the master himself then departed.

However, after a lengthened lapse of time another person came to the store, and affirmed that he had been dispatched by the individual who had locked up and sealed the place with a commission also to collect and lay up a quantity of wheat in the same. And when the keepers of the store saw him, they demanded of him his credentials, in the production of the signet, in order that they might assure themselves of their liberty to open the store to him and to render their obedience to him as to one sent by the person who had sealed the place. And when he could neither exhibit the keys nor produce the credentials of the signet, *for indeed he had no right*, he was thrust out by the keepers, and compelled to flee. For instead of being what he professed to be, he was detected to be a thief and a robber by them, and was convicted and found out through the circumstance that, although, as it seemed, he had taken it into his head to make his appearance a long time after the period that had been determined on beforehand, he yet could neither produce keys, or signet, or any token whatsoever to the keepers, nor display any knowledge of the quantity of corn that was in store: all which things were so many unmistakable proofs that he had not been sent across by the proper owner; and accordingly, as was matter of course, he was forbidden admittance by the keepers.

27. We may give yet another illustration, if it seems good to you. A certain man, the head of a household, and possessed of great riches, was minded to journey abroad for a time, and promised to his sons that he would send them someone who would take his place, and divide among them equally the substance falling to them. And, in truth, not long after that, he did dispatch to them a certain trustworthy and righteous and true man.

And on his arrival, this man took charge of the whole substance, and first of all exerted himself to arrange it and administer it, giving himself great labor in journeying, and even working diligently with his own hands, and toiling like a servant for the good of the estate. Afterwards feeling that his end was at hand, the man wrote out a will, demitting the inheritance to the relations and all the next of kin; and he gave them his seals, and called them together one by one by name, and charged them to preserve the inheritance, and to take care of the substance, and to administer it rightly, even as they had received it, and to take their use of its goods and fruits, as they were themselves left its owners and heirs. If, moreover, any person were to ask to be allowed to benefit by the fruits of this field, they were to show themselves indulgent to such. But if, on the other hand, any one were to declare himself partner in the heirship with them, and were to make his demands on that ground, they were to keep aloof from him, and pronounce him an alien; and further, *they were to hold* that the individual who desired to be received among them ought all the more on that account to do work. Well, then, granting that all these things have been well and rightly disposed of and settled, and that they have continued in that condition for a very long time, how shall we deal with one who presents himself well-nigh three hundred years after, and sets up his claim to the heirship? Shall we not cast him off from us? Shall we not justly pronounce such a one an alien—one who cannot prove himself to have belonged to those related *to our Master*, who never was with our departed Lord in the hour of His sickness, who never walked in the funeral procession of the Crucified, who never stood by the sepulcher, who has no knowledge whatsoever of the manner or the character of His departure, and who, in fine, is now desirous of getting access to the storehouse of corn without presenting any token from him who placed it under lock and seal? Shall we not cast him off from us like a robber and a thief, and thrust him out of our number by all possible means? Yet this man is now in our presence, and fails to produce any of the credentials which we have summarized in what we have already said, and declares that he is the Paraclete whose mission was presignified by Jesus. And by this assertion, in his ignorance perchance, he will make out Jesus Himself to be a liar; for thus He who once said that He would send the Paraclete no long time after, will be proved only to have sent this person, if we accept the testimony which he bears to himself, after an interval of three hundred years and more. In the day of judgment, then, what will those say to Jesus who have departed this life from that time on to the present period? Will they not meet Him with words like these: "Do not punish us rigorously if we have failed to do Thy works. For why, when Thou didst promise to send the Paraclete under Tiberius Cæsar, to convince us of sin and of righteousness, didst Thou send Him only under Probus the Roman emperor, and didst leave us orphaned, not withstanding that Thou didst say, 'I will not leave you comfortless (orphaned),' and after Thou has also assured us that Thou would send the Paraclete presently after Thy departure? What could we orphans do, having no guardian? We have committed no fault; it is Thou that hast deceived us." But away with such a supposition in the case of our Lord Jesus Christ, the Savior of every soul. For He did not confine Himself to mere promises; but when He had once said, "I go to my Father, and I send the Paraclete to you," straightway He sent (that gift of the Paraclete), dividing and imparting the same to His disciples,—bestowing it, however, in greater fulness upon Paul.

28. *Manes said:* You are caught in the charge you yourself bring forward. For you have been speaking now against yourself, and have not perceived that, in trying to cast reproaches in my teeth, you lay yourself under the greater fault. Tell me this now, I pray you: if, as you allege, those who have died from the time of Tiberius on to the days of Probus are to say to Jesus, "Do not judge us if we have failed to do Thy works, for Thou didst not send the Paraclete to us, although Thou didst promise to send Him;" will not those much more use such an address who have departed this life from the time of Moses on to the advent of Christ Himself? And will not those with still greater right express themselves in terms like these: "Do not deliver us over to torments, seeing that we had no knowledge of Thee imparted to us?" And will it only be those that have died thus far previously to His advent who may be seen making such a charge with right? Will not those also do the same who have passed away from Adam's time on to Christ's advent? For none of these either obtained any knowledge of the Paraclete, or received instruction in the doctrine of Jesus. But only this latest generation of men, which has run its course from Tiberius onward, as you make it out, is to be saved: for it is Christ Himself that "has re-deemed them from the curse of the law;" as Paul, too, has given these further testimonies, that "the letter kills, and quicks no man," and that "the law is the ministration of death," and "the strength of sin." *Archelaus said*: You err, not knowing the Scriptures, neither the power of God. For many have also perished after the period of Christ's advent on to this

present period, and many are still perishing,—those, to wit, who have not chosen to devote themselves to works of righteousness; whereas only those who have received Him, and yet receive Him, "have obtained power to become the sons of God." For the evangelist has not said all *have obtained that power*; neither, on the other hand, however, has he put any limit on the time. But this is his expression: "As many as received Him." Moreover, from the creation of the world He has ever been with righteous men, and has never ceased to require their blood *at the hands of the wicked*, from the blood of righteous Abel to the blood of Zacharias. And whence, then, did righteous Abel and all those succeeding worthies, who are enrolled among the righteous, derive their righteousness when as yet there was no law of Moses, and when as yet the prophets had not arisen and discharged the functions of prophecy? Were they not constituted righteous in virtue of their fulfilling the law, "everyone of them showing the work of the law written in their hearts, their conscience also bearing them witness?" For when a man "who has not the law does naturally the things contained in the law, he, not having the law, is a law unto himself." And consider now the multitude of laws thus existing among the several righteous men who lived a life of uprightness, at one time discovering for themselves the law of God implanted in their hearts, at another learning of it from their parents, and yet again being instructed in it further by the ancients and the elders. But inasmuch as only few were able to rise by this medium to the height of righteousness, that is to say, by means of the traditions of parents, when as yet there was no law embodied in writing, God had compassion on the race of man. And was pleased to give through Moses a written law to men, since verily the equity of the natural law failed to be retained in all its perfection in their hearts. In consonance, therefore, with man's first creation, a written legislation was prepared which was given through Moses in behoof of the salvation of very many. For if we reckon that man is justified without the works of the law, and if Abraham was counted righteous, how much more shall those obtain righteousness who have fulfilled the law which contains the things that are expedient for men? And seeing that you have made mention only of three several scriptures, in terms of which the apostle has declared that "the law is a ministration of death," and that "Christ has redeemed us from the curse of the law," and that "the law is the strength of sin," you may now advance others of like tenor, and bring forward any passages which may seem to you to be written against the law, to any extent you please.

29. *Manes said*: Is not that word also to the same effect which Jesus spoke to the disciples, when He was demonstrating those men to be unbelieving: "Ye are of your father the devil, and the lusts of your father ye will do?" By this He means, in sooth, that whatever the wicked prince of this world desired, and whatever he lusted after, he committed to writing through Moses, and by that medium gave it to men for their doing. For "he was a murderer from the beginning, and abode not in the truth, because there is no truth in him. When he speaks a lie, he speaks of his own: for he is a liar, and the father of it." *Archelaus said*: Are you satisfied with what you have already adduced, or have you other statements still to make? *Manes said*: I have, indeed, many things to say, and things of greater weight even than these. But with these I shall content myself. *Archelaus said*: By all

means. Now let us select some instance from among those statements which you allege to be on your side; so that if these be once found to have been properly dealt with, other questions may also be held to rank with them; and if the case goes otherwise, I shall come under the condemnation of the judges, that is to say, I shall have to bear the shame of defeat. You say, then, that the law is a ministration of death, and you admit that "death, the prince of this world, reigned from Adam even to Moses;" for the word of Scripture is this: "even over them that did not sin." *Manes said*: Without doubt death did reign thus, for there is a duality, and these two antagonistic powers were nothing else than both unbegotten. *Archelaus said*: Tell me this then,—how can an unbegotten death take a beginning at a certain time? For "from Adam" is the word of Scripture, and not "before Adam." *Manes said*: But tell me, I ask you in turn, how it obtained its kingdom over both the righteous and the sinful. *Archelaus said*: When you have first admitted that it has had that kingdom from a determinate time and not from eternity, I shall tell you that. *Manes said*: It is written, that "death reigned from Adam to Moses." *Archelaus said*: And consequently it has an end, because it has had a beginning in time. And this saying is also true, that "death is swallowed up in victory." It is apparent, then, that death cannot be unbegotten, seeing that it is shown to have both a beginning and an end. *Manes said*: But in that way it would also follow that God was its maker. *Archelaus said*: By no means; away with such a supposition! "For God made not death; neither hath He pleasure in the destruction of the living." *Manes said*: God made it not; nevertheless it was made, as you admit. Tell us, therefore, from whom it received its empire, or by whom it was created. *Archelaus said*: If I give the most ample proof of the fact that death cannot have the substance of an unbegotten nature, will you not confess that there is but one God, and that an unbegotten God? *Manes said*: Continue your discourse, for your aim is to speak with subtlety. *Archelaus said*: Nay, but you have put forward those allegations in such a manner, as if they were to serve you for a demonstration of an unbegotten root. Nevertheless the positions which we have discussed above may suffice us, for by these we have shown most fully that it is impossible for the substances of two unbegotten natures to exist together.

30. *The judges said*: Speak to those points, Archelaus, which he has just now propounded. *Archelaus said*: By the prince of the world, and the wicked one, and darkness, and death, he means one and the same thing, and alleges that the law has been given by that being, on the ground of the scriptural statement that it is "the ministration of death," as well as on the ground of other things which he has urged against it. Well, then, I say that since, as we have explained above, the law which was written naturally on men's hearts did not keep carefully by the memory of evil things, and since there was not a sufficiently established tradition among the elders, inasmuch as hostile oblivion always attached itself to the memory, and one man was instructed *in the knowledge of that law* by master, and another by himself, it easily came about that transgressions of the law engraved by nature did take place, and that through the violation of the commandments death obtained its kingship among men. For the race of men is of such a nature, that it needs to be ruled by God with a rod of iron. And so death triumphed and reigned with all its power on to Moses, even over

those who had not sinned, in the way which we have explained: over sinners indeed, as these were its proper objects, and under subjection to it,—men after the type of Cain and Judas; but also over the righteous, because they refused to consent to it, and rather withstood it, by putting away from themselves the vices and concupiscence of lusts,—men like those who have arisen at times from Abel on to Zacharias;—death thus always passing, up to the time *of Moses*, upon those after that similitude.

But after Moses had made his appearance, and had given the law to the children of Israel, and had brought into their memory all the requirements of the law, and all that it behooved men to observe and do under it, and when he delivered over to death only those who should transgress the law, then death was cut off from reigning over all men; for it reigned then over sinners alone, as the law said to it, "Touch not those that keep my precepts." Moses therefore served the ministration of this word upon death, while he delivered up to destruction all others who were transgressors of the law; for it was not with the intent that death might not reign in any territory at all that Moses came, inasmuch as multitudes were assuredly held under the power of death even after Moses. And the law was called a "ministration of death" from the fact that then only transgressors of the law were punished, and not those who kept it, and who obeyed and observed the things which are in the law, as Abel did, whom Cain, who was made a vessel of the wicked one, slew. However, even after these things death wished to break the covenant which had been made by the instrumentality of Moses, and to reign again over the righteous; and with this object it did indeed assail the prophets, killing and stoning those who had been sent by God, on to Zacharias. But my Lord

Jesus, as maintaining the righteousness of the law of Moses, was wroth with death for its transgression of the covenant and of that whole ministration, and condescended to appear in the body of man, with the view of avenging not Himself, but Moses, and those who in a continuous succession after him had been oppressed by the violence of death. That wicked one, however, in ignorance *of the meaning* of a dispensation of this kind, entered into Judas, thinking to slay Him by that man's means, as before he had put righteous Abel to death. But when he had entered into Judas, he was overcome with penitence, and hanged himself; for which reason also the divine word says: "O death, where is thy victory? O death, where is thy sting?" And again: "Death is swallowed up of victory." It is for this reason, therefore, that the law is called a "ministration of death" because it delivered sinners and transgressors over to death; but those who observed it, it defended from death; and these it also established in glory, by the help and aid of our Lord Jesus Christ.

31. Listen also to what I have to say on this other expression which has been adduced, viz., "Christ, who redeemed us from the curse of the law." My view of this passage is that Moses, that illustrious servant of God, committed to those who wished to have the right vision, an emblematic law, and also a real law. Thus, to take an example, after God had made the world, and all things that are in it, in the space of six days, He rested on the seventh day from all His works; by which statement I do not mean to affirm that He rested because He was fatigued, but that He did so as having brought to its perfection every creature which He had resolved to introduce. And yet in the sequel it, *the new law*, says:

"My Father worketh hitherto, and I work." Does that mean, then, that He is still making heaven, or sun, or man, or animals, or trees, or any such thing? Nay; but the meaning is, that when these visible objects were perfectly finished, He rested from that kind of work; while, however, He still continues to work at objects invisible with an inward mode of action, and saves men. In like manner, then, the legislator desires also that every individual amongst us should be devoted unceasingly to this kind of work, even as God Himself is; and he enjoins us consequently to rest continuously from secular things, and to engage in no worldly sort of work whatsoever; and this is called our Sabbath. This also he added in the law, that nothing senseless should be done but that we should be careful and direct our life in accordance with what is just and righteous. Now this law was suspended over men, discharging most sharply its curse against those who might transgress it. But because its subjects, too, were but men, and because, as happens also frequently with us, controversies arose and injuries were inflicted, the law likewise at once, and with the severest equity, made any wrong that was done return upon the head of the wrongdoer; so that, for instance, if a poor man was minded to gather a bundle of wood upon the Sabbath, he was placed under the curse of the law, and exposed to the penalty of instant death. The men, therefore, who had been brought up with the Egyptians were thus severely pressed by the restrictive power of the law, and they were unable to bear the penalties and the curses of the law. But, again, He who is ever the Savior, our Lord Jesus Christ, came and delivered those men from these pains and curses of the law, forgiving them their offences. And He indeed did not deal with them as Moses did, putting the severities of the law in force, and granting indulgence to no man for any offence; but He declared that if any man suffered an injury at the hands of his neighbor, he was to forgive him not once only, nor even twice or thrice, nor only seven times, but even unto seventy times seven; but that, on the other hand, if after all this the offender still continued to do such wrong, he ought then, as the last resource, to be brought under the law of Moses, and that no further pardon should be granted to the man who would thus persist in wrong-doing, even after having been forgiven unto seventy times seven. And He bestowed His forgiveness not only on a transgressor of such a character as that, but even on one who did offence to the Son of man. But if a man dealt thus with the Holy Spirit, He made him subject to two curses,—namely, to that of the law of Moses, and to that of His own law; to the law of Moses in truth in this present life, but to His own law at the time of the judgment: for His word is this: "It shall not be forgiven him, neither in this world, neither in the world to come." There is the law of Moses, thus, that in this world gives pardon to no *such* person; and there is the law of Christ that punishes in the future world. From this, therefore, mark how He confirms the law, not only not destroying it, but fulfilling it. Thus, then, He redeemed them from that curse of the law which belongs to the present life; and from this fact has come the appellation "the curse of the law." This is the whole account *which needs be given* of that mode of speech. But, again, why the law is called the "strength of sin," we shall at once explain in brief to the best of our ability. Now it is written that "the law is not made for a righteous man, but for the lawless and disobedient, for the ungodly and for sinners." In these times, then, before Moses, there was no written law for transgressors; whence also Pharaoh, not knowing the strength of sin, transgressed in the way of afflicting the children of Israel with unrighteous burdens, and despised the Godhead, not only himself, but also all who were with him. But, not to make any round-about statement, I shall explain the matter briefly as follows. There were certain persons of the Egyptian race mingling with the people of Moses, when that people was under his rule in the desert; and when Moses had taken his position on the mount, with the purpose of receiving the law, the impatient people, I do not mean those who were the true Israel, but those who had been intermixed with the Egyptians, set up a calf as their god, in accordance with their ancient custom of worshipping idols, with the notion that by such means they might secure themselves against ever having to pay the proper penalties for their iniquities. Thus were they altogether ignorant of the strength of their sin. But when Moses returned (from the mount) and found that out, he issued orders that those men should be put to death with the sword. From that occasion a beginning was made in the correct perception of the strength of sin on the part of these persons through the instrumentality of the law of Moses, and for that reason the law has been called the "strength of sin."

32. Moreover, as to this word which is written in the Gospel, "Ye are of your father the devil," and so forth, we say in brief that there is a devil working in us, whose aim it has been, in the strength of his own will, to make us like himself. For all the creatures that God made, He made very good; and He gave to every individual the sense of free-will, in accordance with which standard He also instituted the law of judgment. To sin is ours, and that we sin not is God's gift, as our will is constituted to

choose either to sin or not to sin. And this you doubtless understand well enough yourself, Manes; for you know that, although you were to bring together all your disciples and admonish them not to commit any transgression or do any unrighteousness, every one of them might still pass by the law of judgment. And certainly whosoever will, may keep the commandments; and whosoever shall despise them, and turn aside to what is contrary to them, shall yet without doubt have to face this law of judgment. Hence also certain of the angels, refusing to submit themselves to the commandment of God, resisted His will; and one of them indeed fell like a flash of lightning upon the earth, while others, harassed by the dragon, sought their felicity in intercourse with the daughters of men, and thus brought on themselves the merited award of the punishment of eternal fire. And that angel who was cast down to earth, finding no further admittance into any of the regions of heaven, now flaunts about among men, deceiving them, and luring them to become transgressors like himself, and even to this day he is an adversary to the commandments of God. The example of his fall and ruin, however, will not be followed by all, inasmuch as to each is given liberty of will. For this reason also has he obtained the name of *devil*, because he has passed over from the heavenly places, and appeared on earth as the disparager of God's commandment. But because it was God who first gave the commandment, the Lord Jesus Himself said to the devil, "Get thee behind me, Satan;" and, without doubt, to go behind God is the sign of being His servant. And again He says, "Thou shalt worship the Lord thy God, and Him only shalt thou serve." Wherefore, as certain men were inclined to yield obedience to his wishes, they were addressed in these terms by the Savior: "Ye are of your father the devil, and the lusts of your father ye will do." And, in fine, when they are found to be actually doing his will, they are thus addressed: "O generation of vipers, who hath warned you to flee from the wrath to come? Bring forth therefore fruits meet for repentance." From all this, then, you ought to see how weighty a matter it is for man to have freedom of will. However, let my antagonist here say whether there is a judgment for the godly and the ungodly, or not. *Manes said*: There is a judgment. *Archelaus said*: I think that what we have said concerning the devil contains no small measure of reason as well as of piety. For every creature, moreover, has its own order; and there is one order for the human race, and another for animals, and another for angels. Furthermore, there is but one only inconvertible substance, the divine substance, eternal and invisible, as is known to all, and as is also borne out by this scripture: "No man hath seen God at any time, save the only begotten Son, which is in the bosom of the Father." All the other creatures, consequently, are of necessity visible,—such as heaven, earth, sea, men, angels, archangels. But if God has not been seen by any man at any time, what consubstantiality can there be between Him and those creatures? Hence we hold that all things whatsoever have, in their several positions, their own proper substances, according to their proper order. You, on the other hand, allege that every living thing which moves is made of one, and you say that every object has received like substance from God, and that this substance is capable of sinning and of being brought under the judgment; and you are unwilling to accept the word which declares that the devil was an angel, and that he fell in transgression, and that he is not of the same substance with God. Logically, you ought to do away with any allowance of the doctrine of a judgment, and that would make it clear which of us is in error. If, indeed, the angel that has been created by God is incapable of falling in transgression, how can the soul, as a part of God, be capable of sinning? But, again, if you say that there is a judgment for sinning souls, and if you hold also that these are of one substance with God; and if still, even although you maintain that they are of the divine nature, you affirm that, notwithstanding that fact, they do not keep the commandments of God, then, even on such grounds, my argument will pass very well, which avers that the devil fell first, on account of his failure to keep the commandments of God. He was not indeed of the substance of God. And he fell, not so much to do hurt to the race of man, as rather to be set at nought by the same. For He "gave unto us power to tread on serpents and scorpions, and over all the strength of the enemy."

33. *The judges said*: He has given demonstration enough of the origin of the devil. And as both sides admit that there will be a judgment, it is necessarily involved in that admission that every individual is shown to have free-will; and since this is brought clearly out, there can be no doubt that every individual, in the exercise of his own proper power of will, may shape his course in whatever direction he pleases. *Manes said*: If (only) the good is from (your) God, as you allege, then you make Jesus Himself a liar. *Archelaus said*: In the first place, admit that the account of what we have adduced is true, and then I will give you proof about the "father of him." *Manes said*: If you prove to me that his father is a liar, and yet show me that for all that you ascribe no such (evil) notion to God, then credit will be given you on all

points. *Archelaus said*: Surely when a full account of the devil has once been presented, and the dispensation set forth, any one now, with an ordinarily vigorous understanding, might simply, by turning the matter carefully over in his own mind, get an idea of who this is that is here called the father of the devil. But though you give yourself out to be the Paraclete, you come very far short of the ordinary sagacity of men. Wherefore, as you have betrayed your ignorance, I shall tell you what is meant by this expression, the "father of the devil." *Manes said*: I say so...; *and he added*: Everyone who is the founder or maker of anything may be called the father, *parent*, of that which he has made. *Archelaus said*: Well, I am verily astonished that you have made so correct an admission in reply to what I have said, and have not concealed either your intelligent apprehension of the affirmation, or the real nature of the same. Now, from this learn who is this father of the devil. When he fell from the kingdom of heaven, he came to dwell upon earth, and there he remained, ever watching and seeking out someone to whom he might attach himself, and whom, through an alliance with himself, he might also make a partner in his own wickedness. Now as long, indeed, as man was not yet existent, the devil was never called either a murderer or a liar together with his father. But subsequently, when man had once been made, and when further he had been deceived by the devil's lies and craftiness, and when the devil had also introduced himself into the body of the serpent, which was the most sagacious of all the beasts, then from that time the devil was called a liar together with his father, and then also the curse was made to rest not only on himself, but also on his father. Accordingly, when the serpent had received him, and had indeed admitted him wholly into its own being, it was, as it were, rendered pregnant, for it bore the burden of the devil's vast wickedness; and it was like one with child, and under the strain of parturition, as it sought to eject the agitations of his malignant suggestions. For the serpent, grudging the glory of the first man, made its way into paradise; and harboring these pains of parturition in itself, it began to produce mendacious addresses, and to generate death for the men who had been fashioned by God, and who had received the gift of life. The devil, however, was not able to manifest himself completely through the serpent; but he reserved his perfection for a time, in order that he might demonstrate it through Cain, by whom he was generated completely. And thus through the serpent, on the one hand, he displayed his hypocrisies and deceits to Eve; while through Cain, on the other hand, he effected the beginning of murder, introducing himself into the firstlings of the "fruits," which that man administered so badly. From this the devil has been called a murderer from the beginning, and also a liar, because he deceived the parties to whom he said, "Ye shall be as gods;" for those very persons whom he falsely declared destined to be gods were afterwards cast out of paradise. Wherefore the serpent which conceived him in its womb, and bore him, and brought him forth to the light of day, is constituted the devil's first father; and Cain is made his second father, who through the conception of iniquities produced pains and parricide: for truly the taking of life was the perpetrating of iniquity, unrighteousness, and impiety all together. Furthermore, all who receive him, and do his lusts, are constituted his brothers. Pharaoh is his father in perfection. Every impious man is made his father. Judas became his father, since he conceived him indeed, though he miscarried: for he did not present a perfect parturition there, since it was really a greater person who was assailed through Judas; and consequently, as I say, it proved an abortion. For just as the woman receives the man's seed, and thereby also becomes sensible of a daily growth within her, so also did Judas make daily advances in evil, the occasions for that being furnished him like seed by the wicked one. And the first seed of evil in him, indeed, was the lust of money; and its increment was theft, for he purloined the moneys which were deposited in the bag. Its offspring, moreover, consisted of less vexations, and compacts with the Pharisees, and the scandalous bargain for a price; yet it was the abortion, and not the birth, that was witnessed in the horrid noose by which he met his death. And exactly in the same way shall it stand also with you: if you bring the wicked one to light in your own deeds, and do his lusts, you have conceived him, and will be called his father; but, on the other hand, if you cherish penitence, and deliver yourself of your burden, you will be like one that brings to the birth. For, as in school exercises, if one gets the subject-matter from the master, and then creates and produces the whole body of an oration by himself, he is said to be the author of the compositions to which he has thus given birth; so he who has taken in any little leaven of evil from the prime evil, is of necessity called the father and procreator of that wicked one, who from the beginning has resisted the truth. The case may be the same, indeed, with those who devote themselves to virtue; for I have heard the most valiant men say to God, "For Thy fear, O Lord, we have conceived in the womb, and we have been in pain, and have brought forth the spirit of salvation." And so those, too, who conceive in respect of the fear of the wicked one, and bring forth the spirit of iniquity, must needs be called the fathers of the same. Thus, on the one hand, they are called sons of that wicked one, so long as they are still yielding obedience to his service; but, on the other hand, they are called fathers if they have attained to the perfection of iniquity. For it is with this view that our Lord says to the Pharisees, "Ye are of your father the devil," thereby making them his sons, as long as they appeared still to be perturbed by him, and meditated in their hearts evil for good toward the righteous. Accordingly, while they deliberated in such a spirit with their own hearts, and while their wicked devices were made chargeable upon themselves, Judas, as the head of all the evil, and as the person who carried out their iniquitous counsels to their consummation, was constituted the father of the crime, having received at their hands the recompense of thirty pieces of silver for his impious cruelty. For "after the sop Satan entered into him" completely. But, as we have said, when his womb was enlarged, and the time of his travail came on, he delivered himself only of an abortive burden in the conception of unrighteousness, and consequently he could not be called the father in perfection, except only at that very time when the conception was still in the womb; and afterwards, when he betook himself to the hangman's rope, he showed that he had not brought it to a complete birth, because remorse followed.

34. I think that you cannot fail to understand this too, that the word "father" is but a single term indeed, and yet one admitting of being understood in various ways. For one is called father, as being the parent of those children whom he has begotten in a natural way; another is called father, as being the guardian of children whom

he has but brought up; and some, again, are called fathers in respect of the privileged standing accruing through time or age. Hence our Lord Jesus Christ Himself is said to have a variety of fathers: for David was called His father, and Joseph was reckoned to be His father, while neither of these two was His father in respect of the actuality of nature. For David is called His father as touching the prerogative of time and age, and Joseph is designated His father as concerning the law of upbringing; but God Himself is His only Father by nature, who was pleased to make all things manifest in short space to us by His word. And our Lord Jesus Christ, making no tarrying, in the space of one year restored multitudes of the sick to health, and gave back the dead to the light of life; and He did indeed embrace all things in the power of His own word. And wherein, forsooth, did He make any tarrying, so that we should have to believe Him to have waited so long, *even to these days*, before He actually sent the Paraclete? Nay, rather, as has been already said above, He gave proof of His presence with us forthwith, and did most abundantly impart Himself to Paul, whose testimony we also believe when he says, "Unto me only is this grace given." For this is he who formerly was a persecutor of the Church of God, but who afterwards appeared openly before all men as a faithful minister of the Paraclete; by whose instrumentality His singular clemency was made known to all men, in such wise that even to us who some time were without hope the largess of His gifts has come. For which of us could have hoped that Paul, the persecutor and enemy of the Church, would prove its defender and guardian? Yea, and not that alone, but that he would become also its ruler, the founder and architect of the churches? Wherefore after him, and after those who were with Himself—that is, the disciples—we are not to look for the advent of any other (such), according to the Scriptures; for our Lord Jesus Christ says of this Paraclete, "He shall receive of mine." Him therefore He selected as an acceptable vessel; and He sent this Paul to us in the Spirit. Into him the Spirit was poured; and as that Spirit could not abide upon all men, but only on Him who was born of Mary the mother of God, so that Spirit, the Paraclete, could not come into any other, but could only come upon the apostles and the sainted Paul. "For he is a chosen vessel," He says, "unto me, to bear my name before kings and the Gentiles." The apostle himself, too, states the same thing in his first epistle, where he says: "According to the grace that is given to me of God, that I should be the minister of Jesus Christ to the Gentiles, ministering the Gospel of God." "I say the truth in Christ, I lie not, my conscience also bearing me witness in the Holy Ghost." And again: "For I will not dare to speak of any of those things which Christ hath not wrought by me by word and deed." "I am the last of all the apostles, that am not meet to be called an apostle. But by the grace of God I am what I am." And it, is his wish to have to deal with those who sought the proof of that Christ who spoke in him, for this reason, that the Paraclete was in him: and as having obtained His gift of grace, and as being enriched with magnificent, honor, he says: "For this thing I besought the Lord thrice, that it might depart from me. And He said unto me, My grace is sufficient for thee; for strength is made perfect in weakness." Again, that it was the Paraclete Himself who was in Paul, is indicated by our Lord Jesus Christ in the Gospel, when He says: "If ye love me, keep my commandments. And I will pray my Father, and He shall give you another Comforter." In these words He points to the Paraclete Himself, for He speaks of "another" Comforter. And hence we have given credit to Paul, and have hearkened to him when he says, "Or seek ye a proof of Christ speaking in me?" and when he expresses himself in similar terms, of which we have already spoken above. Thus, too, he seals his testament for us as for his faithful heirs, and like a father he addresses us in these words in his Epistle to the Corinthians: "I delivered unto you first of all that which I also received, how that Christ died for our sins according to the Scriptures; and that He was buried, and that He rose again the third day according to the Scriptures; and that He was seen of Cephas, then of the eleven apostles: after that He was seen of above five hundred brethren at once; of whom the greater part remain unto this present, but some are fallen asleep. After that He was seen of James; then of all the apostles. And last of all He was seen of me also, as of one born out of due time. For I am the last of the apostles."1796 "Therefore, whether it were I or they, so we preach, and so ye believed." And again, in delivering over to his heirs that inheritance which he gained first himself, he says: "But I fear, lest by any means, as the serpent beguiled Eve through his subtilty, so your minds should be corrupted from the simplicity that is in Christ. For if he that comes preaches another Christ, whom we have not preached, or if ye receive another Spirit, which we have not received, or another gospel, which ye have not accepted, ye might well bear with him. For I suppose that I did nothing less for you than the other apostles."

35. These things, moreover, he has said with the view of showing us that all others who may come after him will be false apostles, deceitful workers, transforming

themselves into the apostles of Christ. And no marvel; for Satan himself is transformed, like an angel of light. What great thing therefore is it, if his ministers also be transformed into the ministers of righteousness?—whose end shall be according to their works. He indicates, further, what manner of men these were, and points out by whom they were being circumvented. And when the Galatians are minded to turn away from the Gospel, he says to them: "I marvel that ye are so soon removed from Him that called you unto another gospel: which is not another; but there be some that trouble you, and would turn you away from the Gospel of Christ. But though we, or an angel from heaven, preach any other gospel unto you than that which has been delivered to you, let him be accursed." And again he says: "To me, who am the least of all the apostles, is this grace given;" and," I fill up that which was behind of the afflictions of Christ in my flesh." And once more, in another place, he declares of himself that he was a minister of Christ more than all others, as though after him none other was to be looked for at all; for he enjoins that not even an angel from heaven is thus to be received. And how, then, shall we credit the professions of this Manes, who comes from Persis, and declares himself to be the Paraclete? By this very thing, indeed, I rather recognize in him one of those men who transform themselves, and of whom the Apostle Paul, that elect vessel, has given us very clear indication when he says: "Now in the last times some shall depart from the faith, giving heed to seducing spirits, and doctrines of devils; speaking lies in hypocrisy; having their conscience seared with a hot iron; forbidding to marry, and *commanding* to abstain from meats, which God hath created to be received with thanksgiving of them which believe and know the truth. For every creature of God is good, and nothing to be refused, if it be received with thanksgiving." The Spirit in the evangelist Matthew is also careful to give note of these words of our Lord Jesus Christ: "Take heed that no man deceive you: for many shall come in my name, saying, I am Christ; and shall deceive many. But if any man shall say unto you, Lo, here is Christ, or there; believe it not. For there shall arise false Christs, and false apostles, and false prophets, and shall show great signs and wonders; insomuch that, if it were possible, they shall deceive the very elect. Behold, I have told you before. If they shall say unto you, Behold, he is in the desert; go not forth: if they shall say, Behold, he is in the secret chambers; believe it not." And yet, after all these directions, this man, who has neither sign nor portent of any kind to show, who has no affinity to exhibit, who never even had a place among the number of the disciples, who never was a follower of our departed Lord, in whose inheritance we rejoice,—this man, I say, although he never stood by our Lord in His weakness, and although he never came forward as a witness of His testament, yea rather, although he never came even within the acquaintance of those who ministered to Him in His sickness, and, in fine, although he obtains the testimony of no person whatsoever, desires us to believe this profession which he makes of being the Paraclete; whereas, even were you to do signs and wonders, we would still have to reckon you a false Christ, and a false prophet, according to the Scriptures. And therefore it is well for us to act with the greater caution, in accordance with the warning which the sainted apostle gives us, when, in the epistle which he wrote to the Colossians, he speaks in the following terms: "Continue in the faith grounded and rooted, and not to be moved away from the hope of the Gospel, which we have heard, and which was preached to every creature which is under heaven." And again: "As ye have therefore received Christ Jesus the Lord, so walk ye in Him; rooted and built up in Him, and stablished in the faith, as ye have been taught, abounding therein with thanksgiving. Beware lest anyone spoil you through philosophy and vain deceit, after the rudiments of the world, and not after Christ. For in Him dwelleth all the fulness of the Godhead." And after all these matters have been thus carefully set forth, the blessed apostle, like a father speaking to his children, adds the following words, which serve as a sort of seal to his testament: "I have fought a good fight, I have finished my course, I have kept the faith: henceforth there is laid up for me a crown of righteousness, which the Lord, the righteous Judge, shall give me at that day; and not to me only, but unto all them also that love His appearing."

36. None of your party, O Manes, will you make a Galatian; neither will you in this fashion divert us from the faith of Christ. Yea, even although you were to work signs and wonders, although you were to raise the dead, although you were to present to us the very image of Paul himself, you would remain accursed still. For we have been instructed beforehand with regard to you: we have been both warned and armed against you by the Holy Scriptures. You are a vessel of Antichrist; and no vessel of honor, in sooth, but a mean and base one, used by him as any barbarian or tyrant may do, who, in attempting to make an inroad on a people living under the righteousness of the laws, sends some select vessel on beforehand, as it were destined to death, with the view of finding out the exact magnitude and character of the strength possessed

by the legitimate king and his nation: for the man is too much afraid to make the inroad himself wholly at unawares, and he also lacks the daring to dispatch any person belonging to his own immediate circle on such a task, through fear that he may sustain some harm. And so it is that your king, Antichrist, has dispatched you in a similar character, and as it were destined to death, to us who are a people placed under the administration of the good and holy King. And this I do not say inconsiderately or without due inquiry; but from the fact that I see you perform no miracle, I hold myself entitled to entertain such sentiments concerning you. For we are given to understand beforehand that the devil himself is to be transformed into an angel of light, and that his servants are to make their appearance in similar guise, and that they are to work signs and wonders, insomuch that, if it were possible, the very elect should be deceived. But who, pray, are you then, to whose lot no such position of kinship has been assigned by your father Satan? For whom have you raised from the dead? What issue of blood do you ever staunch? What eyes of the blind do you ever anoint with clay, and thus cause them to have vision? When do you ever refresh a hungering multitude with a few loaves? Where do you ever walk upon the water, or who of those who dwell in Jerusalem has ever seen you? O Persian barbarian, you have never been able to have a knowledge of the language of the Greeks, or of the Egyptians, or of the Romans, or of any other nation; but the Chaldean tongue alone has been known to you, which verily is not a language prevalent among any great number of people, and you are not capable of understanding any one of another nationality when he speaks. Not thus is it with the Holy Spirit: God forbid; but

He divides to all, and knows all kinds of tongues, and has understanding of all things, and is made all things to all men, so that the very thoughts of the heart cannot escape His cognizance. For what says the Scripture? "That every man heard the apostles speak in his own language through the Spirit, the Paraclete." But why should I say more on this subject? Barbarian priest and crafty coadjutor of Mithras, you will only be a worshipper of the sun god Mithras, who is the illuminator of places of mystic import, as you opine, and the self-conscious deity; that is, you will sport as his worshippers do, and you will celebrate, though with less elegance as it were, his mysteries. But why should I take all this so indignantly? Is it not accordant with all that is fitting, that you should multiply yourself like the tares, until that same mighty father of yours comes, raising the dead, *as he will profess to do*, and persecuting almost to hell itself all those who refuse to yield to his bidding, keeping multitudes in check by that terror of arrogance in which he entrenches himself, and employing threatening against others, and making sport of them by the changing of his countenance and his deceitful dealing? And yet beyond that he shall proceed no further; for his folly shall be made manifest to all men, as was the case with Jamnes and Mambres. *The judges said*: As we have heard now from you, as Paul himself also seems to tell us, and, further, as we have learned likewise from the earlier account given in the Gospel, an introduction to preaching, or teaching, or evangelizing, or prophesying, is not, in this life at least, held out on the same terms to any person in times subsequent *to the apostle's*: and if the opposite appears ever to be the case, the person can only be held to be a false prophet or a false Christ. Now, since you have alleged that the Paraclete was in Paul, and that He attested all things in him, how is it that Paul himself said, "We know in part, and we prophesy in part; but when that which is perfect is come, then that which is in part shall be done away?" What other one did he look for, when he uttered these words? For if he professes himself to be looking for some perfect one, and if someone must needs come, show us who it is of whom he speaks; lest that word of his perchance appear to carry us back to this man, *Manes*, or to him who has sent him, that is to say, Satan, according to your affirmation. But if you admit that that which is perfect is yet to come, then this excludes Satan; and if you look for the coming of Satan, then that excludes the perfect.

37. *Archelaus said*: Those sayings which are put forth by the blessed Paul were not uttered without the direction of God, and therefore it is certain that what he has declared to us is that we are to look for our Lord Jesus Christ as the perfect one, who is the only one that knows the Father, with the sole exception of him to whom He has chosen also to reveal Him, as I am able to demonstrate from His own words. But let it be observed that it is said that when that which is perfect is come, then that which is in part shall be done away. Now this man (Manes) asserts that he is the perfect one. Let him show us, then, what he has done away with; for what is to be done away with is the ignorance which is in us. Let him therefore tell us what he has done away with, and what he has brought into *the sphere of our* knowledge. If he is able to do anything of this nature, let him do it now, in order that he may be believed. These very words of Paul's, if one can but understand them in the full power of their meaning, will only secure entire credit to the statements

made by me. For in that first Epistle to the Corinthians, Paul speaks in the following terms of the perfection that is to come: "Whether there be prophecies, they shall fail; whether there be tongues, they shall cease; whether there be knowledge, it shall be destroyed: for we know in part, and we prophesy in part; but when that which is perfect is come, then that which is in part shall be done away." Observe now what virtue that which is perfect possesses in itself, and of what order that perfection is. And let this man, then, tell us what prophecy of the Jews or Hebrews he has done away with; or what tongues he has caused to cease, whether of the Greeks or of others who worship idols; or what alien dogmas he has destroyed, whether of a Valentinian, or a Marcion, or a Tatian, or a Sabellius, or any others of those who have constructed for themselves their peculiar systems of knowledge. Let him tell us which of all these he has already done away with, or when he is yet to do away with any one of them, in this character of the perfect one. Perchance he seeks some sort of truce—does he? But not thus inconsiderable, not thus obscure and ignoble, will be the manner of the advent of Him who is the truly perfect one, that is to say, our Lord Jesus Christ. Nay, but as a king, when he draws near to his city, does first of all send on before him his lifeguardsmen, his ensigns and standards and banners, his generals and chiefs and prefects, and then forthwith all objects are roused and excited in different fashions, while some become inspired with terror and others with exultation at the prospect of the king's advent; so also my Lord Jesus Christ, who is the truly perfect one, at His coming will first send on before Him His glory, *and* the consecrated heralds of an unstained and untainted kingdom: and then the universal creation will be moved and perturbed, uttering prayers and supplications, until He delivers it from its bondage. And it must needs be that the race of man shall then be in fear and in vehement agitation on account of the many offences it has committed. Then the righteous alone will rejoice, as they look for the things which have been promised them; and the subsistence of the affairs of this world will no longer be maintained, but all things shall be destroyed: and whether they be prophecies or the books of prophets, *they shall fail*; whether they be the tongues of the whole race, they shall cease; for men will no longer need to feel anxiety or to think solicitously about those things which are necessary for life; whether it be knowledge, by what teachers soever it be possessed, it shall also be destroyed: for none of all these things will be able to endure the advent of that mighty King. For just as a little spark, if taken and put up against the splendor of the sun, at once perishes from the view, so the whole creation, all prophecy, all knowledge, all tongues, as we have said above, shall be destroyed. But since the capacities of common human nature are all insufficient to set forth in a few words, and these so weak and so extremely poor, the coming of this heavenly King,—so much so, indeed, that perchance it should be the privilege only of the saintly and the highly worthy to attempt any statement on such a subject,—it may yet be enough for me to *be able to say that I* have advanced what I have now advanced on that theme on the ground of simple necessity,—compelled, as I have been, to do thus much by this person's importunity, and simply with the view of showing you what kind of character he is.

38. And, in good truth, I hold Marcion, and Valentinian, and Basilides, and other heretics, to be

sainted men when compared with this person. For they did display a certain kind of intellect, and they did, indeed, think themselves capable of understanding all Scripture, and did thus constitute themselves leaders for those who were willing to listen to them. But notwithstanding this, not one of these dared to proclaim himself to be either God, or Christ, or the Paraclete, as this fellow has done, who is ever disputing, on some occasions about the ages, and on others about the sun, and how these objects were made, as though he were superior to them himself; for every person who offers an exposition of the method in which any object has been made, puts himself forward as superior to and older than the subject of his discussion. But who may venture to speak of the substance of God, unless, it may be, our Lord Jesus Christ alone? And, indeed, I do not make this statement on the bare authority of my own words, but I confirm it by the authority of that Scripture which has been our instructor. For the apostle addresses the following words to us: "That ye may be lights in this world, holding the word of life for my glory against the day of Christ, seeing that I have not run in vain, neither labored in vain." We ought to understand what is the force and meaning of this saying; for the word may suit the leader, but the effectual work suits the king. And accordingly, as one who looks for the arrival of his king, strives to be able to present all who are under his charge as obedient, and ready, and estimable, and lovely, and faithful, and not less also as blameless, and abounding in all that is good, so that he may himself get commendation from the king, and be deemed by him to be worthy of greater honors, as having rightly governed the province which was entrusted to his administration; so also does the blessed Paul give us to understand our position when he uses these words: "That ye may be as lights in this world, holding the word of life for my glory against the day of Christ." For the meaning of this saying is, that our Lord Jesus Christ, when He comes, will see that his doctrine has proved profitable in us, and that, finding that he, *the apostle*, has not run in vain, neither labored in vain, He will bestow on him the crown of recompense. And again, in the same epistle, he also warns us not to mind earthly things, and tells us that we ought to have our conversation in heaven; from which also we look for the Savior, our Lord Jesus Christ. And as the knowledge of the date of the last day is no secure position for us, he has given us, to that effect, a declaration on the subject in the epistle which he wrote to the Thessalonians, thus: "But of the times and the seasons, brethren, ye have no need that I write unto you; for yourselves know perfectly that the day of the Lord so cometh as a thief in the night." How, then, does this man stand up and try to persuade us to emigrate his opinions, importuning every individual whom he meets to become a Manichæan, and going about and creeping into houses, and endeavoring to deceive minds laden with sins? But we do not hold such sentiments. Nay, rather, we should be disposed to present the things themselves before you all, and bring them into comparison, if it pleases you, with *what we know of* the perfect Paraclete. For you observe that sometimes he uses the interrogative style, and sometimes the deprecatory. But in the Gospel of our Savior it is written that those who stand on the left hand of the King will say: "Lord, when saw we Thee a hungered, or athirst, or naked, or a stranger, or in prison, and did not minister unto Thee?" Thus they will implore Him to be indulgent with them.

But what reply is that righteous Judge and King represented as making to them? "Depart from me into everlasting fire, ye workers of iniquity." He casts them into everlasting fire, although they cease not to direct their entreaties to Him. Do you see, then, *O Manes*, what manner of event that advent of the perfect King is destined to be? Do you not perceive that it will not be such a perfection, *or consummation*, as you allege? But if the great day of judgment is to be looked for after that King, surely this man is greatly inferior to Him. But if he is inferior, he cannot be perfect. And if he is not to be perfect, it is not of him that the apostle speaks. But if it is not of him that the apostle speaks, while he still makes the mendacious statement that it is of himself that the said word *of the apostle* was spoken, then surely he is to be judged a false prophet. Much more, too, might be said to the same effect. But if we were to think of going over in detail all that might thus be adduced, time would fail us for the accomplishment of so large a task. Hence I have deemed it abundantly sufficient thus to have brought under your notice only a few things out of many, leaving the yet remaining portions of such a discussion to those who have the inclination to go through with them.

39. On hearing these matters, those who were present gave great glory to God, and ascribed to Him such praise as it is meet for Him to receive. And on Archelaus himself they bestowed many tokens of honor. Then Marcellus rose up; and casting off his cloak, he threw his arms round Archelaus, and kissed him, and embraced him, and clung to him. Then, too, the children who had chanced to gather about the place began and set the example of pelting Manes and driving him off; and the rest of the crowd followed them, and moved excitedly

about, with the intention of compelling Manes to take to flight. But when Archelaus observed this, he raised his voice like a trumpet above the din, in his anxiety to restrain the multitude, and addressed them thus: "Stop, my beloved brethren, lest mayhap we be found to have the guilt of blood on us at the day of judgment; for it is written of men like this, that 'there must be also heresies among you, that they which are approved may be made manifest among you.'" And when he had uttered these words, the crowds of people were quieted again.—Now, because it was the pleasure of Marcellus that this disputation should have a place given it, and that it should also be described, I could not gainsay his wish, but trusted to the kind consideration of the readers, believing that they would pardon me if my discourse should sound somewhat inartistic or boorish: for the great thing which we have had in view has been, that the means of knowing what took place on this occasion should not fail to be brought within the reach of all who desired to understand the subject. Thereafter, it must be added, when Manes had once taken to flight, he made his appearance nowhere *there again.* His attendant Turbo, however, was handed over by Marcellus to Archelaus; and on Archelaus ordaining him as a deacon, he remained in the suite of Marcellus. But Manes in his flight came to a certain village which was at a considerable distance from the city, and bore the name of Diodorus. Now in that place there was also a presbyter whose name likewise was Diodorus, a man of quiet and gentle disposition, and well reputed both for his faith and for the excellence of his general character. Now when, on a certain day, Manes had gathered a crowd of auditors around him, and was haranguing them, and putting before the people who were present certain outlandish assertions altogether foreign to the tradition of the fathers, and in no way apprehending any opposition that might be made to him on the part of any of these, Diodorus perceived that he was producing some effect by his wickedness, and resolved then to send to Archelaus a letter couched in the following terms:—Diodorus sends greeting to Bishop Archelaus.

40. I wish you to know, most pious father, that in these days there has arrived in our parts a certain person named Manes, who gives out that he is to complete the doctrine of the New Testament. And in the statements which he has made there have been some things, indeed, which may harmonize with our faith; but there have been also certain affirmations of his which seem very far removed from what has come down to us by the tradition of our fathers. For he has interpreted some doctrines in a strange fashion, imposing on them certain notions of his own, which have appeared to me to be altogether foreign and opposed to the faith. On the grounds of these facts I have now been induced to write this letter to you, knowing the completeness and fulness of your intelligence in doctrine, and being assured that none of these things can escape your cognizance. Accordingly, I have also indulged the confident hope that you cannot be kept back by any grudge from explaining these matters to us. As to myself, indeed, it is not possible that I shall be drawn away into any novel doctrine; nevertheless, in behalf of all the less instructed, I have been led to ask a word with your authority. For, in truth, the man shows himself to be a person of extraordinary force of character, both in speech and in action; and indeed his very aspect and attire also bear that out. But I shall here write down for your information some few points which I have been

able to retain in my memory out of all the topics which have been expounded by him: for I know that even by these few you will have an idea of the rest. You well understand, no doubt, that those who seek to set up any new dogma have the habit of very readily perverting into a conformity with their own notions any proofs they desire to take from the Scriptures. In anticipation, however, of this, the apostolic word marks out the case thus: "If anyone preach any other gospel unto you than that which you have received, let him be accursed." And consequently, in addition to what has been once committed to us by the apostles, a disciple of Christ ought to receive nothing new as doctrine. But not to make what I have got to say too long, I return to the subject directly in view. This man then maintained that the law of Moses, to speak shortly, does not proceed from the good God, but from the prince of evil; and that it has no kinship with the new law of Christ, but is contrary and hostile to it, the one being the direct antagonist of the other. When I heard such a sentiment propounded, I repeated to the people that sentence of the Gospel in which our Lord Jesus Christ said of Himself: "I am not come to destroy the law, but to fulfil it." The man, however, averred that He did not utter this saying at all; for he held that when we find that He did abrogate that same law, we are bound to give heed, above all other considerations, to the thing which He actually did. Then he began to cite a great variety of passages from the law, and also many from the Gospel and from the Apostle Paul, which have the appearance of contradicting each other. All this he gave forth at the same time with perfect confidence, and without any hesitation or fear; so that I verily believe he has that serpent as his helper, who is ever our adversary. Well, he declared that there *in the law* God said, "I make the rich man and the poor man;" while here *in the Gospel* Jesus called the poor blessed, and added, that no man could be His disciple unless he gave up all that he had. Again, he maintained that there Moses took silver and gold from the Egyptians when the people fled out of Egypt; whereas Jesus delivered the precept that we should lust after nothing belonging to our neighbor. Then he affirmed that Moses had provided in the law, that an eye should be given in penalty for an eye, and a tooth for a tooth; but that our Lord bade us offer the other cheek also to him who smote the one. He told us, too, that there Moses commanded the man to be punished and stoned who did any work on the Sabbath, and who failed to continue in all things that were written in the law, as in fact was done to that person who, yet being ignorant, had gathered a bundle of sticks on the Sabbath-day; whereas Jesus cured a cripple on the Sabbath, and ordered him then also to take up his bed. And further, He did not restrain His disciples from plucking the ears of corn and rubbing them with their hands on the Sabbath-day, which yet was a thing which it was unlawful to do on the Sabbaths. And why should I mention other instances? For with many different assertions of a similar nature these dogmas of his were propounded with the utmost energy and the most fervid zeal. Thus, too, on the authority of an apostle, he endeavored to establish the position that the law of Moses is the law of death, and that the law of Jesus, on the contrary, is the law of life. For he based that assertion on the passage which runs thus: "In which also may God make us able ministers of the New Testament; not of the letter, but of the spirit: for the letter kills, but the spirit giveth life. But if the ministration of death, engraven in letters on the stones, was made in glory, so that the children of Israel could not steadfastly behold the face of Moses for the glory of his countenance; which glory was to be done away; how shall not the ministration of the Spirit be rather glorious? For if the ministration of condemnation be glory, much more doth the ministration of righteousness exceed in glory. For even that which was made glorious had no glory in this respect, by reason of the glory that excelled. For if that which shall be done away is glorious, much more that which remained is glorious." And this passage, as you are also well aware, occurs in the second Epistle to the Corinthians. Besides, he added to this another passage out of the first epistle, on which he based his affirmation that the disciples of the Old Testament were earthly and natural; and in accordance with this, that flesh and blood could not possess the kingdom of God. He also maintained that Paul himself spoke in his own proper person when he said: "If I build again the things which I destroyed, I make myself a transgressor." Further, he averred that the same apostle made this statement most obviously on the subject of the resurrection of the flesh, when he also said that "he is not a Jew who is one outwardly, neither is that circumcision which is outward in the flesh," and that according to the letter the law has in it no advantage. And again he adduced the statement, that "Abraham has glory, but not before God;" and that "by the law there comes only the knowledge of sin." And many other things did he introduce, with the view of detracting from the honor of the law, on the ground that the law itself is sin; by which statements the simpler people were somewhat influenced, as he continued to bring them forward; and in accordance with all this, he also made use of the affirmation, that "the law and the prophets were until John." He declared, however, that John preached the *true* kingdom of heaven; for verily he held, that by the cutting off of his head it was signified that all who went before him, and who had precedence over him, were to be cut off, and that what was to come after him was alone to be maintained. With reference to all these things, therefore, O most pious Archelaus, send us back a short reply in writing: for I have heard that you have studied such matters in no ordinary degree; and that *capacity which you possess* is God's gift, inasmuch as God bestows these gifts upon those who are worthy of them, and who are His friends, and who show themselves allied to Him in community of purpose and life. For it is our part to prepare ourselves, and to approach the gracious and liberal mind, and forthwith we receive from it the most bountiful gifts. Accordingly, since the learning which I possess for the discussion of themes like these does not meet the requirements of my desire and purpose, for I confess myself to be an unlearned man, I have sent to you, as I have already said more than once, in the hope of obtaining from your hand the amplest solution to this question. May it be well with you, incomparable and honorable father!

41. On receiving this epistle, Archelaus was astonished at the man's boldness. But in the meantime, as the case called for the transmission of a speedy reply, he immediately sent off a letter with reference to the statements made by Diodorus. That epistle ran in the following terms:—

Archelaus sends greeting to the presbyter Diodorus, his honorable son.

## The Acts of the Disposition with the Heresiarch Manes

The receipt of your letter has rejoiced me exceedingly, my dearly beloved friend. I have been given to understand, moreover, that this man, who made his way to me before these days, and sought to introduce a novel kind of knowledge here, different from what is apostolic and ecclesiastical, has also come to you. To that person, indeed, I gave no place: for presently, when we held a disputation together, he was confuted. And I could wish now to transcribe for your behoof all the arguments of which I made use on that occasion, so that by means of these you might get an idea of what that man's faith is. But as that could be done only with leisure at my disposal, I have deemed it requisite, in view of the immediate exigency, to write a short reply to you with reference to what you have written me on the subject of the statements advanced by him. I understand, then, that his chief effort was directed to prove that the law of Moses is not consonant with the law of Christ; and this position he attempted to found on the authority of our Scriptures. Well, on the other hand, not only did we establish the law of Moses, and all things which are written in it, by the same Scripture; but we also proved that the whole Old Testament agrees with the New Testament, and is in perfect harmony with the same, and that they form really one texture, just as a person may see one and the same robe made up of weft and warp together. For the truth is simply this, that just as we trace the purple in a robe, so, if we may thus express it, we can discern the New Testament in the texture of the Old Testament; for we see the glory of the Lord mirrored in the same. We are not therefore to cast aside the mirror, seeing that it shows us the genuine image of the things themselves, faithfully and truly; but, on the contrary, we ought to honor it all the more. Think you, indeed, that the boy who is brought by his pedagogue to the teachers of learning when he is yet a very little fellow, ought to hold that pedagogue in no honor after he has grown up to manhood, simply because he needs his services no longer, but can make his course without any assistance from that attendant to the schools, and quickly find his way to the lecture-rooms? Or, to take another instance, would it be right for the child who has been nourished on milk at first, after he has grown to be capable of receiving stronger meats, then injuriously to spurn the breasts of his nurse, and conceive a horror of them? Nay, rather he should honor and cherish them, and confess himself a debtor to their good services. We may also make use, if it pleases you, of another illustration. A certain man on one occasion having noticed an infant exposed on the ground and already suffering excessively, picked it up, and undertook to rear it in his own house until it should reach the age of youth, and sustained all the toils and anxieties which are wont to fall to the lot of those who have to bring up children. After a time, however, it happened that he who was the child's natural father came seeking the boy, and found him with this person who had brought him up. What ought this boy to do on learning that this is his real father? For I speak, of course, of a boy of the right type. Would he not see to it, that he who had brought him up should be recompensed with liberal gifts; and would he not then follow his natural father, having his proper inheritance in view Even so, then, I think we must suppose that that distinguished servant of God, Moses, in a manner something like this, found a people afflicted by the Egyptians; and he took this people to himself, and nurtured them in the desert like a father, and instructed them like a teacher, and ruled them as a magistrate. This people he also preserved against the coming of him whose people they were. And after a considerable period the father did come, and did receive, his sheep. Now will not that guardian be honored in all things by him to whom he delivered that flock; and will he not be glorified by those who have been preserved by him? Who, then, can be so senseless, my dearly beloved Diodorus, as to say that those are aliens to each other who have been allied with each other, who have prophesied in turn for each other, and who have shown signs and wonders which are equal and similar, the one to the other, and of like nature with each other; or rather, to speak in truth, which belong wholly to the same stock the one with the other? For, indeed, Moses first said to the people: "A Prophet will the Lord our God raise up unto you, like unto me." And Jesus afterwards said: "For Moses spoke of me." You see how these twain give the right hand to each other, although the one was the prophet and the other was the beloved Son, and although in the one we are to recognize the faithful servant, but in the other the Lord Himself. Now, on the other hand, I might refer to the fact, that one who of old was minded to make his way to the schools without the pedagogue was not taken in by the master. For the master said: "I will not receive him unless he accepts the pedagogue." And who the person is, who is spoken of under that figure, I shall briefly explain. There was a certain rich man, who lived after the manner of the Gentiles, and passed his time in great luxury every day; and there was also another man, a poor man, who was his neighbor, and who was unable to procure even his daily bread. It happened that both these men departed this life, that they both descended into the grave, and that the poor man was conveyed into the place of rest, and so forth, as is known to you. But, furthermore, that rich man had also five brothers, living as he too had lived, and disturbed by no doubt as to lessons which they had learned at home from such a master. The rich man then entreated that these should be instructed in the superior doctrine together and at once. But Abraham, knowing that they still stood in need of the pedagogue, said to him: "They have Moses and the prophets." For if they received not these, so as to have their course directed by him, i.e., *Moses*, as by a pedagogue, they would not be capable of accepting the doctrine of the superior master.

42. But I shall also offer, to the best of my ability, some expositions of the other words referred to; that is to say, I shall show that Jesus neither said nor did aught that was contrary to Moses. And first, as to the word, "An eye for an eye, and a tooth for a tooth,"—that is *the expression of* justice. And as to His injunction, that a man, when struck on the one cheek, should offer the other also, that is *the expression of* goodness. Well, then, are justice and goodness opposed to each other? Far from it! There has only been an advance from simple justice to positive goodness. And again, we have the saying, "The workman is worthy of his hire." But if a person seeks to practice any fraud therein, it is surely most just that what he has got possession of by fraud should be required of him, most especially when the hire is large. Now this I say, that when the Egyptians afflicted the children of Israel by the taskmasters who were set over them in the process of making bricks, Moses required and exacted the whole at once, with penalties, within one moment of time. But is this, then, to be called iniquity? Far from it! Surely it is the abstinence of goodness, indeed, when one makes but a moderate use of what is really necessary, and gives up all

that goes beyond that. Let us look, again, at the fact that in the Old Testament we find the words, "I make the rich man and the poor man," whereas Jesus calls the poor blessed. Well, in that saying Jesus did not refer to those who are poor simply in worldly substance, but to those who are poor in spirit, that is to say, who are not inflamed with pride, but have the gentle and lowly dispositions of humility, not thinking of themselves more than they ought to think. This question, however, is one which our adversary has not propounded correctly. For here I perceive that Jesus also looks on willingly at the gifts of the rich men, when they are put into the treasury. All too little, at the same time, is it if gifts are cast into the treasury by the rich alone; and so there are the two mites of the poor widow which are also received with gladness; and in that offering verily something is exhibited that goes beyond what Moses prescribed on the subject of the receipt of moneys. For he received gifts from those who had; but Jesus receives them even from those who have not. But this man says, further, that it is written, that "except a man shall forsake all that he hath, he cannot be my disciple." Well, I observe again, that the centurion, a man exceedingly wealthy and well dowered with worldly influence, possessed a faith surpassing that of all Israel; so that, even if there was anyone who had forsaken all, that man was surpassed in faith by this centurion. But someone may now reason with us thus: It is not a good thing, consequently, to give up riches. Well, I reply that it is a good thing for those who are capable of it; but, at the same time, to employ riches for the work of righteousness and mercy, is a thing as acceptable as though one were to give up the whole at once. Again, as to the assertion that the Sabbath has been abolished, we deny that He has abolished it plainly; for He was Himself also Lord of the Sabbath. And this, *the law's relation to the Sabbath*, was like the servant who has charge of the bridegroom's chamber, and who prepares the same with all carefulness, and does not suffer it to be disturbed or touched by any stranger, but keeps it intact against the time of the bridegroom's arrival; so that when he is come, the same may be used as it pleases himself, or as it is granted to those to use it whom he has bidden enter along with him. And the Lord Jesus Christ Himself gave His testimony to what we affirm, when He said with His heavenly voice, "Can ye make the children of the bridechamber fast so long as the bridegroom is with them?" And again, He did not actually reject circumcision; but we should rather say that He received in Himself and in our stead the cause of circumcision, relieving us by what He Himself endured, and not permitting us to have to suffer any pain to no purpose. For what, indeed, can it profit a man to circumcise himself, if nevertheless he cherishes the worst of thoughts against his neighbor? He desired, accordingly, rather to open up to us the ways of the fullest life by a brief path, lest perchance, after we had traversed lengthened courses of our own, we should find our day prematurely closing upon us in night, and lest, while outwardly indeed we might appear splendid to men's view, we should inwardly be comparable only to ravening wolves, or be likened to whited sepulchers. For far above any person of that type of character is to be placed the man who, although clad only in squalid and threadbare attire, keeps no evil hidden in his heart against his neighbor. For it is only the circumcision of the heart that brings salvation; and that merely carnal circumcision can be of no advantage to men, unless they happen also to be fortified with the spiritual circumcision. Listen also to what Scripture has to say on this subject: "Blessed are the pure in heart, for they shall see God." What need, therefore, is there for me to labor *and suffer*, seeing that I have been made acquainted with the compendious way of life, and know that it shall be mine if only I can be pure in heart? And that is quite in accordance with the truth which we have learned now, to wit, that if one prevails in the keeping of the two commandments, he fulfils the whole law and the prophets. Moreover Paul, the chief of the apostles, after all these sayings, gives us yet clearer instruction on the subject, when he says, "Or seek ye a proof of that Christ who speaks in me?" What have I then to do with circumcision, seeing that I may be justified in uncircumcision? For it is written: "Is any man circumcised? let him not become uncircumcised. Or is any in uncircumcision? let him not be circumcised. For neither of these is anything, but only the keeping of the commandments of God." Consequently, as circumcision is incompetent to save any, it is not greatly to be required, especially when we see that if a man has been called in uncircumcision, and wishes then to be circumcised, he is made forthwith a transgressor of the law. For if I am circumcised, I also fulfil the commandments of the law with the view of being in a position to be saved; but if I am uncircumcised, and remain in uncircumcision, much more in keeping the commandments shall I have life. For I have received the circumcision of the heart, in the spirit, and not that of the letter in the mere ink, in which former there is praise, not of men, but of God. Wherefore let no charge of this kind be brought against me. For just as the man of wealth, who possesses great treasures of gold and silver, so that he gets everything which is necessary for the uses of his house made of these precious metals, has no need to display any vessel of earthenware in anything belonging to his family and yet it does follow from this circumstance that the productions of the potter, or the art of making vessels of pottery, are to be held in abhorrence by him; so also I, who have been made rich by the grace of God, and who have obtained the circumcision of the heart, cannot by any means stand in need of that most profitless *fleshly* circumcision, and yet, for all that, it does not follow that I should call it evil. Far be it from me to do so! If, however, anyone desires to receive still more exact instruction on these matters, he will find them discussed with the greatest fulness in the apostle's first epistle.

43. I shall speak now with the utmost brevity of the veil of Moses and the ministration of death. For I do not think that these things at least can introduce very much to the disparagement of the law. The text in question, then, proceeds thus: "But if the ministration of death, engraven in letters on the stones, was made in glory, so that the children of Israel could not steadfastly behold the face of Moses for the glory of his countenance; which glory was to be done away;" and so on. Well, this passage at any rate acknowledges the existence of a glory on the countenance of Moses, and that surely is a fact favorable to our position. And even although it is to be done away, and although there is a veil in the reading of the same, that does not annoy me or disturb me, provided there be glory in it still. Neither is it the case, that whatever is to be done away is reduced thereby under all manner of circumstances to a condition of dishonor. For when Scripture speaks of glory, it shows us also that it had cognizance of differences in glory. Thus it says:

"There is one glory of the sun, and another glory of the moon, and another glory of the stars: for one star differed from another star in glory." Although then, the sun has a greater glory than the moon, it does not follow that the moon is thereby reduced to a condition of dishonor. And even thus, too, although my Lord Jesus Christ excelled Moses in glory, as the lord excelled the servant, it does not follow from this that the glory of Moses is to be scorned. For in this way, too, we are able to satisfy our hearers, as the nature of the word itself carries the conviction with it in that we affirm what we allege on the authority of the Scriptures themselves, or verily make the proof of our statements all the clearer also by illustrations taken from them. Thus, although a person kindles a lamp in the night-time, after the sun has once risen he has no further need of the paltry light of his lamp, on account of that effulgence of the sun which sends forth its rays all the world over; and yet, for all that, the man does not throw his lamp contemptuously away, as if it were something absolutely antagonistic to the sun; but rather, when he has once found out its use, he will keep it with all the greater carefulness. Precisely in this way, then, the law of Moses served as a sort of guardian to the people, like the lamp, until the true Sun, who is our Savior, should arise, even as the apostle also says to us: "And Christ shall give thee light." We must look, however, to what is said further on: "Their minds were blinded: for until this day remained the same veil in the reading of the Old Testament; it is untaken away, because it is done away in Christ. For even unto this day, when Moses is read, the veil is upon their heart. Nevertheless, when it shall turn to the Lord, the veil shall be taken away. Now the Lord is that Spirit." What, then, is meant by this? Is Moses present with us even unto this day? Is it the case that he has never slept, that he has never gone to his rest, that he has never departed this life? How is it that this phrase "unto this day" is used here? Well, only mark the veil, which is placed, where he says it is placed, on their hearts in their reading. This, therefore, is the word of censure upon the children of Israel, because they read Moses and yet do not understand him, and refuse to turn to the Lord; for it is He that was prophesied of by Moses as about to come. This, then, is the veil which was placed upon the face of Moses, and this also is his testament; for he says in the law: "A prince shall not be wanting from Judah, nor a leader from his thighs, until He come whose he is; and He will be the expectation of the nations: who shall bind His foal unto the vine, and His ass's colt unto the choice vine; He shall wash His garments in wine, and His clothes in the blood of grapes; His eyes shall be suffused with wine, and His teeth white with milk;" and so on. Moreover, he indicated who He was, and whence He was to come. For he said: "The Lord God will raise up unto you a Prophet from among your brethren, like unto me: unto Him hearken ye." Now it is plain that this cannot be understood to have been said of Jesus the son of Nun. For there is nothing of this circumcision found in him. After him, too, there have still been kings from Judah; and consequently this prophecy is far from being applicable to him. And this is the veil which is on Moses; for it was not, as some among the unlearned perhaps fancy, any piece of linen cloth, or any skin that covered his face. But the apostle also takes care to make this plain to us, when he tells us that the veil is put on in the reading of the Old Testament, inasmuch as they who are called Israel from olden time still look for the coming of Christ, and perceive not that the princes have been wanting from Judah, and the leaders from his thighs; as even at present we see them in subjection to kings and princes, and paying tribute to these, without having any power left to them either of judgment or of punishment, such as Judah certainly had, for after he had condemned Thamar, he was able also to justify her. "But you will also see your life hang (in doubt) before your eyes."

44. Now this word also has the veil. For up to the time of Herod they did appear to retain a kingdom in some sort; and it was by Augustus that the first enrolment took place among them, and that they began to pay tribute, and to be rated. Now it was also from the time when our Lord Jesus Christ began to be prophesied of and looked for that there began to be princes from Judah and leaders of the people; and these, again, failed just at the approach of His advent. If, then, the veil is taken away which is put on in that reading of theirs, they will understand the true virtue of the circumcision; and they will also discover that the generation of Him whom we preach, and His cross, and all the things that have happened in the history of our Lord, are those very matters which had been predicted of that Prophet. And I could wish, indeed, to examine every such passage of Scripture by itself, and to point out its importance, as it is meet that it should be understood. But as it is another subject that is now urgent, these passages shall be discussed by us at some season of leisure. For at present, what I have already said may be sufficient for the purpose of showing, that it is not without reason that the veil is (said to be) put upon the heart of certain persons in the reading of the Old Testament. But those who turn to the Lord shall have the veil taken away from them. What

precise force all these things, however, may possess, I leave to the apprehension of those who have sound intelligence. Let us come now again to that word of Moses, in which he says: "The Lord your God shall raise up a Prophet unto you, of your brethren, like unto me." In this saying I perceive a great prophecy delivered by the servant Moses, as by one cognizant that He who is to come is indeed to be possessed of greater authority than himself, and nevertheless is to suffer like things with him, and to show like signs and wonders. For there, Moses after his birth was placed by his mother in an ark, and exposed beside the banks of the river; here, our Lord Jesus Christ, after His birth by Mary His mother, was sent off in flight into Egypt through the instrumentality of an angel. There, Moses led forth his people from the midst of the Egyptians, and saved them; and here, Jesus, leading forth His people from the midst of the Pharisees, transferred them to an eternal salvation. There, Moses sought bread by prayer, and received it from heaven, in order that he might feed the people with it in the wilderness; here, my Lord Jesus by His own power satisfied with five loaves five thousand men in the wilderness. There, Moses when he was tried was set upon the mountain and fasted forty days; and here, my Lord Jesus was led by the Spirit into the wilderness when He was tempted of the devil, and fasted in like manner forty days. There, before the sight of Moses, all the first-born of the Egyptians perished on account of the treachery of Pharaoh; and here, at the time of the birth of Jesus, every male among the Jews suddenly perished by reason of the treachery of Herod. There, Moses prayed that Pharaoh and his people might be spared the plagues; and here, our Lord Jesus prayed that the Pharisees might be pardoned, when He said, "Father, forgive them, for they know not what they do." There, the countenance of Moses shone with the glory of the Lord, so that the children of Israel could not steadfastly look upon his face, on account of the glory of his countenance; and here, the Lord Jesus Christ shone like the sun, and His disciples were not able to look upon His face by reason of the glory of His countenance and the intense splendor of the light. There, Moses smote down with the sword those who had set up the calf; and here, the Lord Jesus said, "I came to send a sword upon the earth, and to set a man at variance with his neighbor," and so on. There, Moses went without fear into the darkness of the clouds that carry water; and here, the Lord Jesus walked with all power upon the waters. There, Moses gave his commands to the sea; and here, the Lord Jesus, when he was on the sea, rose and gave His commands to the winds and the sea. There, Moses, when he was assailed, stretched forth his hands and fought against Amalek;and here, the Lord Jesus, when we were assailed and were perishing by the violence of that erring spirit who works now in the just, stretched forth His hands upon the cross, and gave us salvation. But there are indeed many other matters of this kind which I must pass by, my dearly beloved Diodorus, as I am in haste to send you this little book with all convenient speed; and these omissions of mine you will be able yourself to supply very easily by your own intelligence. Write me, however, an account of all that this servant of the adversary's cause may do hereafter. May the Omnipotent God preserve you whole in soul and in spirit!

45. On receipt of this letter, Diodorus made himself master of its contents, and then entered the lists against Manes. This he did too with such spirit, that he

was commended greatly by all for the careful and satisfactory demonstration which he gave of the fact that there is a mutual relationship between the two testaments, and also between the two laws. Discovering also more arguments for himself he was able to bring forward many points of great pertinency and power against the man, and in defense of the truth. He also reasoned in a conclusive manner against his opponent on verbal grounds. For example, he argued with him in the following manner:—Did you say that the testaments are two? Well, then, say either that there are two old testaments, or that there are two new testaments. For you assert that there are two unbegottens belonging to the same time, or rather eternity: and if there are in this way two, there should be either two old testaments or two new testaments. If, however, you do not allow this, but affirm, on the contrary, that there is one old testament and that there is also another new testament, that will only prove again that there is but one author for both; and the very sequence will show that the Old Testament belongs to Him to whom also the New Testament pertains. We may illustrate this by the case of a man who says to some other individual, Lease me your old house. For by such a mode of address does he not pronounce the man to be also the owner of a new house? Or, on the other hand, if he says to him, Show me your new house; does he not by that very word designate him also as the possessor of an old house? Then, again, this also is to be considered, that since there are two beings, having an unbegotten nature, it is also necessary from that to suppose each of them to have (what must be called) an old testament, and thus there will appear to be two old testaments; if indeed you affirm that both these beings are ancient, and both indeed without a beginning. But I have not learned doctrine like that; neither do the Scriptures contain it. You, however, who allege that the law of Moses comes from the prince of evil, and not from the good God, tell me who those were who withstood Moses to the face—I mean Jamnes and Mambres? For, every object that withstands, withstands not itself, but some other one, either better or worse; as Paul also gives us to understand when he writes in the following terms in his second Epistle to Timothy: "As Jamnes and Mambres withstood Moses, so have these also resisted the truth: men of corrupt mind, reprobate concerning the faith. But they shall proceed no further: for their folly is manifest unto all men, as theirs also was." Do you observe how he compares Jamnes and Mambres to men of corrupt mind, and reprobate concerning the faith; while he likens Moses, on the other hand, to the truth? But the holy John, the greatest of the evangelists, also tells us of the giving and diffusing of grace for grace; for he indicates, indeed, that we have received the law of Moses out of the fulness of Christ, and he means that for that one grace this other grace has been made perfect in us through Jesus Christ. It was also to show this to be the case that our Lord Jesus Christ Himself spoke in these terms: "Do not think that I will accuse you to the Father: there is one that accuses you, even Moses, in whom ye hope. For had ye believed Moses, ye would indeed have believed me: for he wrote of me. But if ye believe not his writings, how shall ye believe my words?" And besides all these words, there are still many other passages that might be adduced both from the Apostle Paul and from the Gospels, by which we are able to prove that the old law belongs to no other one than that Lord to whom also the new testament appertains, and which it would suit us very well to set forth, and to make use of in a satisfactory manner. Now, however, the evening prevents us from doing so; for the day is drawing to its close, and it is right that we should now bring our disputation to an end. But an opportunity will be given you to-morrow to put questions to us on any points you are pleased to take up. And after these words they went their way.

46. Next morning, however, Archelaus suddenly made his appearance at this residence in which Diodorus was staying, before anyone was yet stirring abroad. Manes accordingly, all unconscious of the fact that Archelaus was now on the spot again, challenged Diodorus publicly to engage in a disputation with him; his intention being to crush him with a verbal display, because he perceived that he was a man of a simple nature, and not very deeply learned in questions concerning the Scriptures. For he had now had a taste of the doctrine of Archelaus. When, therefore, the multitudes had again collected in the place usually set apart for the disputation, and when Manes had just begun to reason, all on a sudden Archelaus appeared among them, and embraced Diodorus, and saluted him with an holy kiss. Then truly were Diodorus, and all those who were present, filled with wonder at the dispensation of divine providence which thus provided that Archelaus should arrive among them at the very time when the question was *just* raised; for in reality, as must be confessed, Diodorus, with all his religiousness, had been somewhat afraid of the conflict. But when Manes caught sight of Archelaus, he at once drew back from his insulting attitude; and with his pride cast down not a little, he made it quite plain that he would gladly flee from the contest. The multitude of hearers, however, looked upon the arrival of Archelaus as

something like the advent of an apostle, because he had shown himself so thoroughly furnished, and so prompt and ready for a defense *of the truth* by speech. Accordingly, after demanding silence from the people by a wave of his right hand,—*for no inconsiderable tumult had arisen*,—Archelaus began an address in the following terms:—Although some amongst us have gained the honor of wisdom and the meed of glory, yet this I beg of you, that you retain in your minds the testimony of those things which have been said before my arrival. For I know and am certain, brethren, that I now take the place of Diodorus, not on account of any impossibilities attaching to him, but because I came to know this person here at a previous time, when he made his way with his wicked designs into the parts where I reside, by the favor of Marcellus, that man of illustrious name, whom he endeavored to turn aside from our doctrine and faith, with the object, to wit, of making him an effective supporter of this impious teaching. Nevertheless, in spite of all his plausible addresses, he failed to move him or turn him aside from the faith in any one particular. For this most devout Marcellus was only found to be like the rock on which the house was built with the most solid foundations; and when the rain descended, and the floods and the winds burst in and beat upon that house, it stood firm: for it had been built on the most solid and immoveable foundations. And the attempt thus made by this person who is now before you, brought dishonor rather than glory upon himself. Moreover, it does not seem to me that he can be very excusable if he proves to be ignorant of what is in the future; for surely he ought to know beforehand those who are on his own side: certainly he should have this measure of knowledge, if it be true indeed that the Spirit of the Paraclete dwells in him. But inasmuch as he is really a person blinded with the darkness of ignorance, he ran in vain when he journeyed to Marcellus, and he did but show himself to be like the stargazer, who busies himself with describing things celestial, while all the time he is ignorant of what is passing in his own home. But lest it should appear as if I were setting aside the question in hand by speaking in this strain, I shall now refrain from such discourse. And I shall also give this man the privilege of taking up any point which may suit him best as a commencement to any treatment of the subject and the question. And to you, as I have said already, I only address the request that ye be impartial judges, so as to give to him who speaks the truth the proper honor and the palm.

47. Then Manes, after silence had been secured among all, thus began his address: Like others, Archelaus, you too smite me with the most injurious words, notwithstanding that my sentiments on the subject of God are correct, and that I hold also a proper conception of Christ; and yet the family of the apostles is rather of the character that bears all things and endures all things, even although a man may assail them with reviling and curses. If it is your intention to persecute me, I am prepared for it: and if you wish to involve me in punishment, I shall not shrink from it; yea, if you mean even to put me to death, I am not afraid: "For we ought to fear Him only who is able to destroy both soul and body in hell." *Archelaus said*: Far be that from me! Not such is my intention. For what have you ever had to suffer at my hands, or at the hands of those who think with us, even when you were disparaging us and doing us injury, and when you were speaking in detraction of the traditions of our fathers, and

when it was your aim to work the death of the souls of men that were well established in the truth, and that were kept with the most conscientious carefulness; for which, in truth, the whole wealth of the world would not serve as a sufficient compensation? Nevertheless, what grounds have you for assuming this position? What have you to show? Tell us this,—what signs of salvation have you to bring before us? For the bare bravado of words will not avail to satisfy the multitude here present, neither will it be enough to qualify them for recognizing which of us holds the knowledge of the truth the more correctly. Wherefore, as you have got the opportunity of speaking first, tell us first to what particular head of the subject you wish us to direct the disputation. *Manes said*: If you do not offer a second time an unfair resistance to the positions which shall be stated with all due propriety by us, I shall speak with you; but if you mean to show yourself still in the character which on a former occasion I perceived you to take up, I shall address myself to Diodorus, and shall keep clear of your turbulence. *Archelaus said*: I have already expressed my opinion that we shall be simply abusing the occasion by the mere bandying of empty words. If any one on one side is found to offer an unfair resistance, leave that to the decision of the judges. But now, tell us what you have got to advance. *Manes said*: If you do not mean a second time merely to gainsay the positions which are stated with all due correctness by me, I shall begin. *Archelaus said*: "If not this," and "if not that," are ways of speaking which mark out an ignorant man. You are ignorant, therefore, of what is in the future. But as to this particular thing which you do declare to be still future, to gainsay or not to gainsay is a matter in my own power. How, then, will that argument about the two trees stand, in which you place your trust as in a buckler of the most approved strength? For if I am of the contrary side, how do you require my obedience? And if, on the other hand, there is in me the disposition of obedience, how are you so greatly alarmed lest I should gainsay you? For you maintain that evil remains evil always, and that good remains good always, in utter ignorance of the force of your words. *Manes said*: Have I employed you as the advocate of my words, so that you may determine also the intelligence that may suit my knowledge? And how will you be able to explain what belongs to another person, when you cannot make what pertains to yourself clear? But if Diodorus now admits himself to be vanquished, my reasonings will then be addressed to you. If, however, he still stands out, and is prepared to speak, I beg you to give over and cease from interfering with the substantiating of the truth. For you are a strange sheep; nevertheless hereafter you will be introduced into the number of the same flock, as the voice of Jesus also intimates,—that Jesus, namely, who appeared in the form of man indeed, and yet was not a man. *Archelaus said*: Are you not, then, of opinion that He was born of the Virgin Mary? *Manes said*: God forbid that I should admit that our Lord Jesus Christ came down to us through the natural womb of a woman! For He gives us His own testimony that He came down from the Father's bosom; and again He says, "He that receives me, receives Him that sent me;" and, "I came not to do mine own will, but the will of Him that sent me;" and once more, "I am not sent but unto the lost sheep of the house of Israel." And there are also innumerable other passages of a similar import, which point Him out as one that *came*, and not as one that was *born*. But if you are greater than He, and if you know better than He what is true, how do we yet believe Him? *Archelaus said*: Neither am I greater than He, for I am His servant nor can I be even the equal of my Lord, for I am His unprofitable servant; I am a disciple of His words, and I believe those things which have been spoken by Him, and I affirm that they are unchangeable. *Manes said*: A certain person somewhat like you once said to Him, "Mary Thy mother, and Thy brethren, stand without;" and He took not the word kindly, but rebuked the person who had uttered it, saying, "Who is my mother, and who are my brethren?" And He showed that those who did His will were both His mothers and His brethren. If you, however, mean to say that Mary was actually His mother, you place yourself in a position of considerable peril. For, without any doubt, it would be proved on the same principles that He had brethren also by her. Now tell me whether these brethren were begotten by Joseph or by the same Holy Spirit. For if you say that they were begotten by the same Holy Spirit, it will follow that we have had many Christs. And if you say that these were not begotten by the same Holy Spirit, and yet aver that He had brethren, then without doubt we shall be under the necessity of understanding that, in succession to the Spirit and after Gabriel, the most pure and spotless virgin formed an actual marriage connection with Joseph. But if this is also a thing altogether absurd—I mean the supposition that she had any manner of intercourse with Joseph—tell me whether then He had brethren. Are you thus to fix the crime of adultery also on her, most sagacious Marcellus? But if none of these suppositions suits the position of the Virgin undefiled, how will you make it out that He had brothers? And if you are unable to prove clearly to us that He had brethren, will it be any the easier for you to prove Mary to be His mother, in accordance with the saying of him who ventured to write, "Behold, Thy mother and Thy brethren stand without?" Yet, although that man was bold enough to address Him thus, no one can be mightier or greater than this same person Himself who shows us His mother or His brethren. Nay, He does not deign even to hear it said that He is David's son. The Apostle Peter, however, the most eminent of all the disciples, was able to acknowledge Him on that occasion, when all were putting forth the several opinions which they entertained respecting Him: for he said, "Thou art the Christ, the Son of the living God;" and immediately He names him blessed, addressing him thus: "For my heavenly Father hath revealed it unto thee." Observe what a difference there is between these two words which were spoken by Jesus. For to him who had said, "Behold, Thy mother stands without," He replied, "Who is my mother, or who are my brethren?" But to him who said, "Thou art the Christ the Son of the living God," He makes the return of a beatitude and benediction. Consequently, if you will have it that He was born of Mary, then it follows that no less than Peter, He is Himself thus proved to have spoken falsely. But if, on the other hand, Peter states what is true, then without doubt that former person was in error. And if the former was in error, the matter is to be referred back to the writer. We know, therefore, that there is one Christ, according to the Apostle Paul, whose words, as in consonance at least with His advent, we believe.

48. On hearing these statements, the multitudes assembled were greatly moved, as if they felt that these reasonings gave the correct account of the truth, and that Archelaus could have nothing to urge against them; for

this was indicated by the commotion which arose among them. But when the crowd of auditors became quiet again, Archelaus made answer in the following manner: No one, truly, shall ever be able to prove himself mightier than the voice of our Lord Jesus Christ, neither is there found any name equal to His, as it is written: "Wherefore God hath exalted Him, and given Him a name which is above every name." Nor, again, in the matter of testimony can anyone ever be equal to Him; and accordingly I shall simply adduce the testimonies of His own voice in answer to you,—first of all, indeed, with the view of solving those difficulties which have been enunciated by you, so that you may not say, as is your wont to do, that these are matters which are not in harmony with the Person Himself. Now, you maintain that the man who brought the word to Jesus about His mother and His brethren was rebuked by Him as if he was in error, as the writer was in error. Well, I affirm that neither was this person rebuked who brought Him the message about His mother and His brethren, nor was Peter only named blessed above him; but each of these two parties received from Him the answer that was properly called forth by their several utterances, as the discourse will demonstrate in what follows. When one is a child, he thinks as a child, he speaks as a child; but when he becomes a mature man, those things are to be done away which are proper for a child: in other words, when one reaches forth unto those things which are before, he will forget those which are behind. Hence, when our Lord Jesus Christ was engaged in teaching and healing the race of men, so that all pertaining to it might not utterly perish together, and when the minds of all those who were listening to Him were intently occupied with these interests, it made an interruption altogether inopportune when this messenger came in and put Him in mind of His mother and His brethren. What then? Ought He, now, yourself being judge, to have left those whom He was healing and instructing, and gone to speak with His mother and His brethren? Would you not by such a supposition at once lower the character of the Person Himself? When, again, He chose certain men who were laden and burdened with sins for the honor of discipleship, to the number of twelve, whom He also named His apostles, He gave them this injunction, Leave father and mother, that you may be made worthy of me; intending by this that thence forward the memory of father or mother should no more impair the steadfastness of their heart. And on another occasion, when a different individual chose to say to Him, "I will go and bury my father," He answered, "Let the dead bury their dead." Behold, then, how my Lord Jesus Christ edifies His disciples unto all things necessary, and delivers His sacred words to everyone, in due accordance with what is meet for him. And just in the same way, too, on this other occasion, when a certain person came in with the inconsiderate message about His mother, He did not embrace the occurrence as an opportunity for leaving His Father's commission unattended to even for the sake of having His mother with Him. But in order to show you still more clearly that this is the real account of the matter, let me remind you that Peter, on a certain season, subsequent to the time of his receiving that declaration of blessedness from Him, said to Jesus, "Be it far from Thee, Lord: this shall not be unto Thee." This he said after Jesus had announced to him that the Son of man must go up to Jerusalem, and be killed, and rise again the third day. And in answer then to Peter He said: "Get thee behind me,

Satan; for thou savors not the things that be of God, but those that be of men." Now, since it is your opinion that the man who brought the message about His mother and His brethren was rebuked by Jesus, and that he who said a little before, "Thou art the Christ, the Son of the living God," obtained the word of blessing, mark you that Jesus (may be said to have) rather preferred that person to whom He condescended to give the more gracious and indulgent answer; whereas Peter, even after that benediction, now got no appellation expressive of indulgence addressed to him, by reason of his having failed carefully to observe the nature of the announcement that was made to him. For the error of that messenger was at once corrected by the tenor of the reply; but the dullness of this apostle's apprehension was condemned with a severer rebuke. And from this you may perceive that the Lord Jesus, observing what was proper and opportune with regard to the interrogations thus addressed to Him, gave to each the reply that was worthy of it, and suited to it. But supposing that, as you say, Peter was pronounced blessed on the ground of his having said what was true, and that that messenger was reproved on account of the error he committed, tell me then why it is, that when the devils confessed Him, and said, "We know Thee, who Thou art, the holy God," He rebuked them, and commanded them to be silent? Why was it not the case, if He does indeed take pleasure in the testimonies borne to Him by those who confess Him, that He recompensed them also with benedictions, as He did to Peter when he gave utterance to the truth? But if that would be an absurd supposition, it only remains that we must understand the words spoken by Him always in accordance with the place, the time, the persons, the subjects, and the due consideration of the circumstances. For only this method will save us from falling into the error of pronouncing rashly on His sayings, and thus making ourselves liable to merited chastisement: and this will also help me to make it more and more intelligible to you, that the man who brought the tidings of His mother was much rather the person honored. However, in forgetfulness of the subject which was proposed to us for discussion, you have turned off to a different theme. Nevertheless listen to me for a brief space. For if you choose, indeed, to consider those words somewhat more carefully, we shall find that the Lord Jesus displayed great clemency in the case of the former of these two parties; and this I shall prove to you by illustrations suited to your capacity. A certain king who had taken up arms, and gone forth to meet an enemy, was earnestly considering and planning how he might subdue those hostile and foreign forces. And when his mind was occupied with many cares and anxieties, after he had forced his way among his adversaries, and when, further, as he began afterwards to make captives of them, the anxious thought was now also pressing upon him as to how he might secure the safety and interests of those who had toiled with him, and borne the burden of the war, a certain messenger broke inopportunely in upon him, and began to remind him of domestic matters. But he was astonished at the man's boldness, and at his unseasonable suggestions, and thought of delivering such a fellow over to death. And had that messenger not been one who was able to appeal to his tenderest affections in bringing the news that it was well with those at home, and that all went on prosperously and successfully there, that punishment might have been his instant and well-merited doom. For what else should be a king's care, so long as the time of war endures, than to provide for the safety of the people of his province, and to look after military matters? And even thus it also was that that messenger came inopportunely in upon my Lord Jesus Christ, and brought the report about His mother and His brethren unseasonably, just when He was fighting against ills which had assailed the very citadel of the heart, and when He was healing those who for a long time had been under the power of diverse infirmities, and when He had now put forth His utmost effort to secure the salvation of all. And truly that man might have met with a sentence like that pronounced on Peter, or even one severer still. But the hearing of the name of His mother and His brethren drew forth His clemency.

49. But in addition to all that has been said already, I wish to adduce still further proof, so that all may understand what impiety is contained in this assertion of yours. For if your allegation is true, that He was not born, then it will follow undoubtedly that He did not suffer; for it is not possible for one to suffer who was not also born. But if He did not suffer, then the name of the cross is done away with. And if the cross was not endured, then Jesus did not rise from the dead. And if Jesus rose not from the dead, then no other person will rise again. And if no one shall rise again, then there will be no judgment. For it is certain that, if I am not to rise again, I cannot be judged. But if there is to be no judgment, then the keeping of God's commandments will be to no purpose, and there will be no occasion for abstinence: nay, we may say, "Let us eat and drink, for tomorrow we shall die." For all these consequences follow when you deny that He was born of Mary. But if you acknowledge that He was born of Mary, then His passion

will necessarily follow, and His resurrection will be consequent on His passion, and the judgment on His resurrection: and thus the injunctions of Scripture will have their proper value for us. This is not therefore an idle question, but there are the mightiest issues involved in this word. For just as all the law and the prophets are summed up in two words, so also all our hope is made to depend on the birth by the blessed Mary. Give me therefore an answer to these several questions which I shall address to you. How shall we get rid of these many words of the apostle, so important and so precise, which are expressed in terms like the following: "But when the good pleasure of God was with us, He sent His Son, made of a woman;" and again, "Christ our Passover is sacrificed for us;" and once more, "God hath both raised up the Lord, and will raise up us together with Him by His own power?" And there are many other passages of a similar import; as, for example, this which follows: "How say some among you, that there is no resurrection of the dead? For if there be no resurrection of the dead, then is not Christ risen: and if Christ be not risen, then is our preaching vain. Yea, and we shall be found false witnesses of God; who have testified against God that He raised up Christ: whom He raised not up. For if the dead rise not, then is not Christ risen: and if Christ be not raised, your faith is vain; ye are yet in your sins. Then they also which are fallen asleep in Christ are perished. If in this life only we have hope in Christ, we are more miserable than all men. But now is Christ risen from the dead, the beginning of them that sleep;" and so on. Who, then, I ask, can be found so rash and audacious as not to make his faith fit in with these sacred words, in which there is no qualification nor any dubiety? Who, I ask you,

O foolish Galatian, has bewitched you, as those were bewitched "before whose eyes Jesus Christ was evidently set forth, crucified?" From all this I think that these testimonies should suffice in proof of the judgment, and the resurrection, and the passion; and the birth by Mary is also shown to be involved naturally and at once in these facts. And what matters it though you refuse to acquiesce in this, when Scripture proclaims the fact most unmistakeably? Nevertheless I shall again put a question to you, and let it please you to give me an answer. When Jesus gave His testimony concerning John, and said, "Among them that are born of women there hath not risen a greater than John the Baptist: notwithstanding, he that is less in the kingdom of heaven is greater than he," tell me what is meant by there being a greater than he in the kingdom of heaven. Was Jesus less in the kingdom of heaven than John? I say, God forbid! Tell me, then, how this is to be explained, and you will certainly surpass yourself. Without doubt *the meaning is, that* Jesus was less than John among those that are born of woman; but in the kingdom of heaven He is greater than he. Wherefore tell me this too, O Manichæus: If you say that Christ was not born of Mary, but that He only appeared like a man, while yet He was not really a man, the appearance being effected and produced by the power that is in Him, tell me, I repeat, on whom then was it that the Spirit descended like a dove? Who is this that was baptized by John? If He was perfect, if He was the Son, if He was the Power, the Spirit could not have entered into Him; just as a kingdom cannot enter within a kingdom. And whose, too, was that voice which was sent forth out of heaven, and which gave Him this testimony, "This is my beloved Son, in whom I am well pleased?" Come, tell me; make no delay; who is this that acquires all these things, that does all these things? Answer me: Will you thus audaciously adduce blasphemy for reason, and will you attempt to find a place for it?

50. *Manes said*: No one, certainly, who may be able to give a reply to what has just been alleged by you need fear incurring the guilt of blasphemy, but should rather be deemed thoroughly worthy of all commendation. For a true master of his art, when any matters are brought under his notice, ought to prepare his reply with due care, and make all clearly to understand the points that are in question or under doubt; and most especially ought he to do so to uninstructed persons. Now since the account of our doctrine does not satisfy you, be pleased, like a thorough master of your art, to solve this question also for me in a reasonable manner. For to me it seems but pious to say that the Son of God stood in need of nothing whatsoever in the way of making good His advent upon earth; and that He in no sense required either the dove, or baptism, or mother, or brethren, or even mayhap a father,—which father, however, according to your view, was Joseph; but that He descended altogether by Himself alone, and transformed Himself, according to His own good pleasure, into *the semblance of* a man, in accordance with that word of Paul which tells us that "He was found in fashion as a man." Show me, therefore, what thing He could possibly need who was able to transform Himself into all manner of appearances. For when He chose to do so, He again transformed this human fashion and mien into the likeness of the sun. But if you gainsay me once more, and decline to acknowledge that I state the faith correctly, listen to my definition of the position in which you stand. For if you say that He was only man *as born* of

Mary, and that He received the Spirit at His baptism, it will follow that He will be made out to be Son by increase and not by nature. If, however, I grant you to say that He is Son according to increase, and that He was made as a man, your opinion is that He is really a man, that is to say, one who is flesh and blood. But then it will necessarily follow that the Spirit also who appeared like a dove was nothing else than a natural dove. For the two expressions are the same,—namely, "as a man" and "like a dove;" and consequently whatever may be the view you take of the one passage which uses the phrase "as a man," you ought to hold that same view also of this other passage in which the expression "like a dove" is used. It is a clear matter of necessity to take these things in the same way, for only thus can we find out the real sense of what is written concerning Him in the Scriptures. *Archelaus said*: As you cannot do so much for yourself, like a thorough master of your art, so neither should I care to put this question right and with all patience to make it clear, and to give the evident solution of the difficulty, were it not for the sake of those who are present with us, and who listen to us. For this reason, therefore, I shall also explain the answer that ought to be given to this question as it may be done most appropriately. It does not seem to you, then, to be a pious thing to say that Jesus had a mother in Mary; and you hold a similar view on certain other positions which you have now been discussing in terms which I, for my part, altogether shrink from repeating. Now, sometimes a master of any art happens to be compelled by the ignorance of an opponent both to say and to do things which time would *make him* decline; and accordingly, because the necessity is laid upon me, by consideration for the multitude present, I may give a brief answer to those statements which have been made so erroneously by you. Let us suppose, now, your allegation to be that if we understand Jesus to be a man made of Mary after the course of nature, and regard him consequently as having flesh and blood, it will be necessary also to hold that the Holy Spirit was a real dove, and not a spirit. Well, then, how can a real dove enter into a real man, and abide in him? For flesh cannot enter into flesh. Nay rather, it is only when we acknowledge Jesus to be a true man, and also hold him who is there said to be like a dove to be the Holy Spirit, that we shall give the correct account according to reason on both sides. For, according to right reason, *it may be said that* the Spirit dwells in a man, and descends upon him, and abides in him; and these, indeed, are things which have happened already in all due competence, and the occurrence of which is always possible still, as even you yourself *admit, inasmuch as you* did aforetime profess to be the Paraclete of God, you flint, as I may call you, and no man, so often forgetful of the very things which you assert. For you declared that the Spirit whom Jesus promised to send has come upon you; and whence can He come but by descending from Heaven? And if the Spirit descends thus on the man worthy of Him, then verily must we fancy that real doves descended upon you? Then truly should we rather discover in you the thieving dove-merchant, who lays snares and lines for the birds. For surely you well deserve to be made a jest of with words of ridicule. However, I spare you, lest perchance I appear to offend the auditors by such expressions, and also most especially because it is beside my purpose to throw out against you all that you deserve to hear said about you. But let me return to the proper subject. For I am mindful of that transformation of

## The Acts of the Disposition with the Heresiarch Manes

thine, in virtue of which you say that God has transformed Himself into *the fashion of* a man or *into that of* the sun, by which position you think to prove that our Jesus was made man only in fashion and in appearance; which assertion may God save any of the faithful from making. Now, for the rest, that opinion of yours would reduce the whole matter to a dream, so far as we are concerned, and to mere figures; and not that only, but the very name of an advent would be done away: for He might have done what He desired to do, though still seated in heaven, if He is, as you say, a spirit, and not a true man. But it is not thus that "He humbled Himself, and took the form of a servant;" and I say this of Him who was made man of Mary. For what? Might not we, too, have set forth things like those with which you have been dealing, and that, too, all the more easily and the more broadly? But far be it from us to swerve one jot or one tittle from the truth. For He who was born of Mary is the Son, who chose of His own accord to sustain this mighty conflict,—namely, Jesus. This is the Christ of God, who descended upon him who is of Mary. If, however, you refuse to believe even the voice that was heard from heaven, all that you can bring forward in place of the same is but some rashness of your own; and though you were to declare yourself on that, no one would believe you. For forthwith Jesus was led by the Spirit into the wilderness to be tempted by the devil; and as the devil had no correct knowledge of Him, he said to Him, "If thou be the Son of God." Besides, he did not understand the reason of this bearing of the Son of God *by Mary*, who preached the kingdom of heaven, whose was also indeed a great tabernacle, and one that could not have been prepared by any other: whence, too, He who was nailed to the cross, on rising again from the dead, was taken up thither where Christ the Son of God reigned; so that when He begins to conduct His judgment, those who have been ignorant of Him shall look on Him whom they pierced. But in order to secure your credence, I propose this question to you: Why was it, that although His disciples sojourned a whole year with Him, not one of them fell prostrate on his face before Him, as you were saying a little ago, save only in that one hour when His countenance shone like the sun? Was it not by reason of that tabernacle which had been made *for Him* of Mary? For just as no other had the capacity sufficient for sustaining the burden of the Paraclete except only the disciples and the blessed Paul, so also no other was able to bear the Spirit who descended from heaven, and through whom that voice of the Father gave its testimony in these terms, "This is my beloved Son," save only He who was born of Mary, and who is above all the saints,— namely, Jesus. But now give us your answer to those matters which I bring forward against you. If you hold that He is man only in mien and form, how could He have been laid hold of and dragged off to judgment by those who were born of man and woman—to wit, the Pharisees—seeing that a spiritual body cannot be grasped by bodies of grosser capacities? But if you, who as yet have made no reply to the arguments brought before you, have now any kind of answer to offer to the word and proposition I have adduced, proceed, I pray you, and fetch me at least a handful or some fair modicum of your sunlight. But that very sun, indeed, inasmuch as it is possessed of a more subtle body, is capable of covering and enveloping you; while you, on the other hand, can do it no injury, even although you were to trample it under foot. My Lord Jesus, however, if He was laid hold of, was laid hold of as a man by men. If He is not a man, neither was He laid hold of. If He was not laid hold of, neither did He suffer, nor was He baptized. If He was not baptized, neither is any of us baptized. But if there is no baptism, neither will there be any remission of sins, but every man will die in his own sins. *Manes said*: Is baptism, then, given on account of the remission of sins? *Archelaus said*: Certainly. *Manes said*: Does it not follow, then, that Christ has sinned, seeing that He has been baptized? *Archelaus said*: God forbid! Nay, rather, He was made sin for us, taking on Him our sins. For this reason He was born of a woman, and for this reason also He approached the rite of baptism, in order that He might receive the purification of this part, and that thus the body which He had taken to Himself might be capable of bearing the Spirit, who had descended in the form of a dove.

51. When Archelaus had finished this speech, the crowds of people marveled at the truth of his doctrine, and expressed their vehement commendations of the man with loud outcries, so that they exerted themselves most energetically, and would have kept him from his return. Thereafter, however, they withdrew. After some time, again, when they were gathered together, Archelaus persuaded them to accede to his desire, and listen quietly to the word. And among his auditors were not only those who were with Diodorus, but also all who were present from his province and from the neighboring districts. When silence, then, was secured, Archelaus proceeded to speak to them of Manes in the following manner: You have heard, indeed, what is the character of the doctrine which we teach, and you have got some proof of our faith; for I have expounded the Scriptures before you all,

precisely in accordance with the views which I myself have been able to reach in studying them. But I entreat you now to listen to me in all silence, while I speak with the utmost possible brevity, with the view of giving you to understand who this person is who has made his appearance among us, and whence he comes, and what character he has, exactly as a certain man of the name of Sisinius, one of his comrades, has indicated the facts to me; which individual I am also prepared, if it please you, to summon in evidence of the statements I am about to make. And, in truth, this person did not decline to affirm the very same facts which we now adduce, even when Manes was present; for the above-mentioned individual became a believer of our doctrine, as did also another person who was with me, named Turbo. Accordingly, all that these parties have conveyed in their testimony to me, and also all that we ourselves have discovered in the man, I shall not suffer to be kept back from your cognizance.

Then, indeed, the multitudes became all the more excited, and crowded together to listen to Archelaus; for, in good sooth, the statements which were made by him offered them the greatest enjoyment. Accordingly, they earnestly urged him to tell them all that he pleased, and all that he had on his mind; and they declared themselves ready to listen to him there and then, and engaged to stay on even to the evening, and until the lights should be lit.

Stimulated therefore by their heartiness, Archelaus began his address with all confidence in the following terms:—My brethren, you have heard, indeed, the primary causes relating to my Lord Jesus,—I mean those which are decided out of the law and the prophets; and of the subsidiary causes also relating to my Lord Jesus Christ, our Savior, you are not ignorant. And why should I say more? From the loving desire for the Savior we have been called Christians, as the whole world itself attests, and as the apostles also plainly declare. Yea, further, that best master-builder of His, Paul himself, has laid our foundation, that is, the foundation of the Church and has put us in trust of the law, ordaining ministers, and presbyters, and bishops in the same, and describing in the places severally assigned to that purpose, in what manner and with what character the ministers of God ought to conduct themselves, of what repute the presbyters ought to be possessed, and how they should be constituted, and what manner of persons those also ought to be who desire the office of bishop. And all these institutions, which were once settled well and rightly for us, preserve their proper standing and order with us to this day, and the regular administration of these rules abides amongst us still. But as to this fellow, Manes by name, who has at present burst boastfully forth upon us from the province of Persia, and between whom and me disputation has now for the second time been stirred, I shall tell you about his lineage, and that, too, in all fulness; and I shall also show you most lucidly the source from which his doctrine has descended. This man is neither the first nor the only originator of this type of doctrine. But a certain person belonging to Scythia, bearing the name Scythianus, and living in the time of the apostles, was the founder and leader of this sect, just as many other apostates have constituted themselves founders and leaders, who from time to time, through the ambitious desire of arrogating positions of superior importance to themselves, have given out falsehoods for the truth, and have perverted the simpler class of people to their own lustful appetencies, on whose names and treacheries, however, time does not permit us at present to descant. This Scythianus, then, was the person who introduced this self-contradictory dualism; and for that, too, he was himself indebted to Pythagoras, as also all the other followers of this dogma have been, who all uphold the notion of a dualism, and turn aside from the direct course of Scripture: but they shall not gain any further success therein.

52. No one, however, has ever made such an unblushing advance in the promulgation of these tenets as this Scythianus. For he introduced the notion of a feud between the two unbegottens, and all those other fancies which are the consequences of a position of that kind. This Scythianus himself belonged to the stock of the Saracens, and took as his wife a certain captive from the Upper Thebaid, who persuaded him to dwell in Egypt rather than in the deserts. And would that he had never been received by that province, in which, as he dwelt in it for a period, he found the opportunity for learning the wisdom of the Egyptians! for, to speak truth, he was a person of very decided talent, and also of very liberal means, as those who knew him have likewise testified in accounts transmitted to us. Moreover, he had a certain disciple named Terebinthus, who wrote four books for him. To the first of these books he gave the title of the *Mysteries*, to the second that of the *Heads*, to the third that of the *Gospel*, and to the last of all that of the *Treasury*. He had these four books, and this one disciple whose name was Terebinthus. As, then, these two persons had determined to reside alone by themselves for a considerable period, Scythianus thought of making an excursion into Judea, with the purpose of meeting with all those who had a reputation there as teachers; but it came to pass that he suddenly departed this life soon after that,

without having been able to accomplish anything. That disciple, moreover, who had sojourned with him had to flee, and made his way toward Babylonia, a province which at present is held by the Persians, and which is distant now a journey of about six days and nights from our parts. On arriving there, Terebinthus succeeded in giving currency to a wonderful account of himself, declaring that he was replete with all the wisdom of the Egyptians, and that he was really named now, not Terebinthus, but another Buddas, and that this designation had been put upon him. He asserted further that he was the son of a certain virgin, and that he had been brought up by an angel on the mountains. A certain prophet, however, of the name of Parcus, and Labdacus the son of Mithras, charged him with falsehood, and day after day unceasingly they had keen and elevated contentions on this subject. But why should I speak of that at length? Although he was often reproved, he continued, nevertheless, to make declarations to them on matters which were antecedent to the world, and on the sphere, and the two luminaries; and also on the question whither and in what manner the souls depart, and in what mode they return again into the bodies; and he made many other assertions of this nature, and others even worse than these,—as, for instance, that war was raised with God among the elements, that the prophet himself might be believed. However, as he was hard pressed for assertions like these, he betook himself to a certain widow, along with his four books: for he had attached to himself no disciple in that same locality, with the single exception of an old woman who became an intimate of his. Then, on a subsequent occasion, at the earliest dawn one morning, he went up to the top of a certain house, and there began to invoke certain names, which Turbo has told us only the seven elect have learned. He ascended to the housetop, then, with the purpose of engaging in some religious ceremony, or some art of his own; and he went up alone, so as not to be detected by any one: for he considered that, if he was convicted of playing false with, or holding of little account, the religious beliefs of the people, he would be liable to be punished by the real princes of the country. And as he was revolving these things then in his mind, God in His perfect justice decreed that he should be thrust beneath earth by a spirit; and forthwith he was cast down from the roof of the house; and his body, being precipitated lifeless to the ground, was taken up in pity by the old woman mentioned above, and was buried in the wonted place of sepulture.

53. After this event all the effects which he had brought with him from Egypt remained in her possession. And she rejoiced greatly over his death, and that for two reasons: first, because she did not regard his arts with satisfaction; and secondly, because she had obtained such an inheritance, for it was one of great value. But as she was all alone, she bethought herself of having someone to attend her; and she got for that purpose a boy of about seven years of age, named Corbicius, to whom she at once gave his freedom, and whom she also instructed in letters. When this boy had reached his twelfth year the old woman died, and left to him all her possessions, and among other things those four books which Scythianus had written, each of them consisting of a moderate number of lines. When his mistress was once buried, Corbicius began to make his own use of all the property that had been left him. Abandoning the old locality, he took up his abode in the middle of the city, where the king

## The Acts of the Disposition with the Heresiarch Manes

of Persia had his residence; and there altering his name, he called himself Manes instead of Corbicius, or, to speak more correctly, not Manes, but Mani: for that is the kind of inflection employed in the Persian language. Now, when this boy had grown to be a man of well-nigh sixty years of age, he had acquired great erudition in all the branches of learning taught in those parts, and I might almost say that in these he surpassed all others. Nevertheless he had been a still more diligent student of the doctrines contained in these four books; and he had also gained three disciples, whose names were Thomas, Addas, and Hermas. Then, too, he took these books, and transcribed them in such wise that he introduced into them much new matter which was simply his own, and which can be likened only to old wives' fables. Those three disciples, then, he thus had attached to him as conscious participants in his evil counsels; and he gave, moreover, his own name to the books, and deleted the name of their former owner, as if he had composed them all by himself. Then it seemed good to him to send his disciples, with the doctrines which he had committed to writing in the books, into the upper districts of that province, and through various cities and villages, with the view of securing followers. Thomas accordingly determined to take possession of the regions of Egypt, and Addas those of Scythia, while Hermas alone chose to remain with the man himself. When these, then, had set out on their course, the king's son was seized with a certain sickness; and as the king was very anxious to see him cured, he published a decree offering a large reward, and engaging to bestow it upon anyone who should prove himself capable of restoring the prince. On the report of this, *all at haphazard*, like the men who are accustomed to play the game of cubes, which is another name for the dice, Manes presented himself before the king, declaring that he would cure the boy. And when the king heard that, he received him courteously, and welcomed him heartily. But not utterly to weary my hearers with the recital of the many things which he did, let me simply say that the boy died, or rather was bereft of life, in his hands. Then the king ordered Manes to be thrust into prison, and to be loaded with chains of iron weighing half a hundred weight. Moreover, those two disciples of his who had been sent to inculcate his doctrine among the different cities were also sought for with a view to punishment. But they took to flight, without ever ceasing, however, to introduce into the various localities which they visited that teaching of theirs which is so alien to the faith, and which has been inspired only by Antichrist.

54. But after these events they returned to their master, and reported what had befallen them; and at the same thee they got an account of the numerous ills which had overtaken him. When, therefore, they got access to him, as I was saying, they called his attention to all the sufferings they had had to endure in each several region; and as for the rest, they urged it upon him that regard ought now to be had to the question of safety; for they had been in great terror lest any of the miseries which were inflicted on him should fall to their own lot. But he counselled them to fear nothing, and rose to harangue them. And then, while he lay in prison, he ordered them to procure copies of the books of the law of the Christians; for these disciples who had been dispatched by him through the different communities were held in execration by all men, and most of all by those with whom the name

of Christians was an object of honor. Accordingly, on receiving a small supply of money, they took their departure for those districts in which the books of the Christians were published; and pretending that they were Christian messengers, they requested that the books might be shown them, with a view to their acquiring copies. And, not to make a lengthened narrative of this, they thus got possession of all the books of our Scriptures, and brought them back with them to their master, who was still in prison. On receiving these copies, that astute personage set himself to seek out all the statements in our books that seemed to favor his notion of a dualism; which, however, was not really his notion, but rather that of Scythianus, who had promulgated it a long time before him. And just as he did in disputing with me, so then too, by rejecting some things and altering others in our Scriptures, he tried to make out that they advanced his own doctrines, only that the name of Christ was attached to them there. That name, therefore, he pretended on this account to assume to himself, in order that the people in the various communities, hearing the holy and divine name of Christ, might have no temptation to execrate and harass those disciples of his. Moreover, when they came upon the word which is given us in our Scriptures touching the Paraclete, he took it into his head that he himself might be that Paraclete; for he had not read with sufficient care to observe that the Paraclete had come already,—namely, at the time when the apostles were still upon earth. Accordingly, when he had made up these impious inventions, he sent his disciples also to proclaim these fictions and errors with all boldness, and to make these false and novel words known in every quarter. But when the king of Persia learned this fact, he prepared to inflict condign punishment upon him. Manes, however, received information of the king's intention, having been warned of it in sleep, and made his escape out of prison, and succeeding in taking to flight, for he had bribed his keepers with a very large sum of money. Afterwards he took up his residence in the castle of Arabion; and from that place he sent by the hand of Turbo the letter which he wrote to our Marcellus, in which letter he intimated his intention of visiting him. On his arrival there, a contest took place between him and me, resembling the disputation which you have observed and listened to here; in which discussion we sought to show, as far as it was in our power, that he was a false prophet. I may add, that the keeper of the prison who had let him escape was punished, and that the king gave orders that the man should be sought for and apprehended wherever he might be found. And as these things have come under my own cognizance, it was needful that I should also make the fact known to you, that search is being made for this fellow even to the present day by the king of Persia.

55. On hearing this, the multitude wished to seize Manes and hand him over to the power of those foreigners who were their neighbors, and who dwelt beyond the river Stranga, especially as also some time before this certain parties had come to seek him out; who, however, had to take their leave again without finding any trace of him, for at that time he was in flight. However, when Archelaus made this declaration, Manes at once took to flight, and succeeded in making his escape good before anyone followed in pursuit of him. For the people were detained by the narrative which was given by Archelaus, whom they heard with great pleasure; nevertheless some of them did follow in close pursuit after him. But he made

again for the roads by which he had come, and crossed the river, and effected his return to the castle of Arabion. There, however, he was afterwards apprehended and brought before the king, who, being inflamed with the strongest indignation against him, and fired with the desire of avenging two deaths upon him,—namely, the death of his own son, and the death of the keeper of the prison,—gave orders that he should be flayed and hung before the gate of the city, and that his skin should be dipped in certain medicaments and inflated; his flesh, too, he commanded to be given as a prey to the birds. When these things came under the knowledge of Archelaus at a later period, he added *an account of* them to the former discussion, so that all the facts might be made known to all, even as I, who have written narrative of these matters, have explained the circumstances in what precedes. And all the Christians, therefore, having assembled, resolved that the decision should be given against him transmitting that as a sort of epilogue to his death which would be in proper consonance with the other circumstances of his life. Besides that, Archelaus added words to the following effect:—My brethren, let none of you be incredulous in regard to the statements made by me: I refer to the assertion that Manes was not himself the first author of this impious dogma, but that it was only made public by him in certain regions of the earth. For assuredly that man is not at once to be reckoned the author of anything who has simply been the bearer of it to some quarter or other, but only he has a right to that credit who has been the discoverer of it. For as the helmsman who receives the ship which another has built, may convey it to any countries he pleases, and yet he remains one who has had nothing to do with the construction of the vessel, so also is this man's position to be understood. For he did not impart its origin to this matter really from the beginning; but he was only the means of transmitting to men what had been discovered by another, as we know on the evidence of trustworthy testimonies, on the ground of which it has been our purpose to prove to you that the invention of this wickedness did not come from Manes, but that it originated with another, and that other indeed a foreigner, who appeared a long time before him. And further, that the dogma remained unpublished for a time, until at length the doctrines which had thus been lying in obscurity for a certain period were brought forward publicly by him as if they were his own, the title of the writer having been deleted, as I have shown above. Among the Persians there was also a certain promulgator of similar tenets, one Basilides, of more ancient date, who lived no long time after the period of our apostles. This man was of a shrewd disposition himself, and as he observed that at that time all other subjects were preoccupied, he determined to affirm that same dualism which was maintained also by Scythianus. And as, in fine, he had nothing to advance which was properly his own, he brought the sayings of others before his adversaries. And all his books contain some matters at once difficult and extremely harsh. The thirteenth book of his *Tractates*, however, is still extant, which begins in the following manner: "In writing the thirteenth book of our *Tractates*, the wholesome word furnished us with the necessary and fruitful word." Then he illustrates how it, *the antagonism between good and evil*, is produced under the figures of a rich principle and a poor principle, of which the latter is by nature without root and without place, and only supervenes upon things. This is the only topic which the book contains. Does it not then contain a strange word; and, as certain parties have been thus minded, will ye not also all be offended with the book itself, which has such a beginning as this?—But Basilides, returning to the subject after an introduction of same five hundred lines, more or less, proceeds thus: "Give up this vain and curious variation, and let us rather find out what inquiries the foreigners have instituted on the subject of good and evil, and what opinions they have been led to adopt on all these subjects. For certain among them have maintained that there are for all things two beginnings, to which they have referred good and evil, holding that these beginnings are without beginning and ungenerate; that is to say, that in the origins of things there were light and darkness, which existed of themselves, and which were not merely declared to exist. While these subsisted by themselves, they led each its own proper mode of life, such as it was its will to lead, and such as was competent to it; for in the case of all things, what is proper to any one is also in amity with the same, and nothing seems evil to itself. But after they came to know each other, and after the darkness began to contemplate the light, then, as if fired with a passion for something superior to itself, the darkness pressed on to have intercourse with the light."

A Fragment of the Same Disputation.

*The fragment is introduced by Cyril in the following terms:* —He, i.e., *Manes*, fled from prison and came into Mesopotamia; but there he was met by that buckler of righteousness, Bishop Archelaus. And in order to bring him to the test in the presence of philosophical judges, this person convened an assembly of Grecian auditors, so as to preclude the possibility of its being alleged that the judges were partial, as might have been the case had they been Christians. *Then the matter proceeded as we shall now indicate:—*

1. Archelaus said to Manes: Give us a statement now of the doctrines you promulgate.—Thereupon the man, whose mouth was like an open sepulcher, began at once with a word of blasphemy against the Maker of all things, saying: The God of the Old Testament is the inventor of evil, who speaks thus of Himself: "I am a consuming fire."—But the sagacious Archelaus completely undid this blasphemy. For he said: If the God of the Old Testament, according to your allegation, calls Himself a fire, whose son is He who says, "I am come to send fire upon the earth?" If you find fault with one who says, "The Lord kills and makes alive," why do you honor Peter, who raised Tabitha to life, but also put Sapphira to death? And if again, you find fault with the one because He has prepared a fire, why do you not find fault with the other, who says, "Depart from me into everlasting fire?" If you find fault with Him who says, "I, God, make peace, and create evil," explain to us how Jesus says, "I came not to send peace, but a sword." Since both persons speak in the same terms, one or other of these two things must follow: namely, either they are both good because they use the same language; or, if Jesus passes without censure though He speaks in such terms, you must tell us why you reprehend Him who employs a similar mode of address in the Old Testament.

2. Then Manes made the following reply to him: And what manner of God now is it that blinds one? For it is Paul who uses these words: "In whom the God of this

world hath blinded the minds of them which believe not, lest the light of the Gospel should shine in them." But Archelaus broke in and refuted this very well, saying: Read, however, a word or two of what precedes that sentence, namely, "But if our Gospel be hid, it is hid in them that are lost." You see that it is hidden in them that are lost. "For it is not meet to give the holy things to dogs." And furthermore, is it only the God of the Old Testament that has blinded the minds of them who believe not? Nay, has not Jesus Himself also said: "Therefore speak I to them in parables: that seeing, they may not see?" Is it then because He hated them that He desired them not to see? Or is it *not* on account of their unworthiness, since they closed their own eyes? For wherever wickedness is a matter self-chosen, there too there is the absence of grace. "For unto him that hath shall be given, but from him that hath not shall be taken away even that which he seemed to have."

3. But even although we should be under the necessity of accepting the exegesis advocated by some,— for the subject is not altogether unworthy of notice,—and of saying thus, that He hath actually blinded the minds of them that believe not, we should still have to affirm that He hath blinded them for good, in order that they may recover their sight to behold things that are holy. For it is not said that He hath blinded their soul, but only that He hath blinded the minds of them that believe not. And that mode of expression means something like this: Blind the whorish mind of the whore-monger, and the man is saved; blind the rapacious and thievish mind of the thief and the man is saved. But do you decline to understand the sentence thus? Well, there is still another interpretation. For the sun blinds those who have bad sight; and those

who have watery eyes are also blinded when they are smitten by the light: not, however, because it is of the nature of the sun to blind, but because the eye's own constitution is not one of correct vision. And in like manner, those whose hearts are afflicted with the ailment of unbelief are not capable of looking upon the rays *of the glory* of the Godhead. And again, it is not said, "He hath blinded their minds lest they should hear the Gospel," but rather "lest the light of the glory of the Gospel of our Lord Jesus Christ should shine unto them." For to hear the Gospel is a thing committed to all; but the glory of the Gospel of Christ is imparted only to the sincere and genuine. For this reason the Lord spoke in parables to those who were incapable of hearing, but to His disciples He explained these parables in private. For the illumination of the glory is for those who have been enlightened, while the blinding is for them who believe not. These mysteries, which the Church now declares to you who are transferred from the lists of the catechumens, it is not her custom to declare to the Gentiles. For we do not declare the mysteries touching the Father, and the Son, and the Holy Spirit to a Gentile; neither do we speak of the mysteries plainly in presence of the catechumens; but many a time we express ourselves in an occult manner, so that the faithful who have intelligence may apprehend the truths referred to, while those who have not that intelligence may receive no hurt.

Elucidations.

I.

Oh that "foolish and unlearned questions" had been avoided, as Scripture bids! Surely, we should be as decent about the conjugal relations of the Blessed Virgin as we are socially in all such matters. Pearson, as in the note, says all that should be said on such a subject. Photius, in his thirtieth epistle, expounds the text Matt. i. 25. But it did not rest there. Let it rest here.

II.

I adopt the views of those who reverently suppose that when it was said, "Let us make man," etc., Lucifer conceived rebellion, and said, "This be far from Thee, Lord;" fearing the creature made in God's own image might outshine himself. Hence our Lord applies the epithet "Satan" to Peter when he ventures to use similar language. Possibly there lurks a reference to this in such language as Job iv. 18. I have previously referred to the *Messias and Anti-Messias* of the Rev. Charles Ingham Black (London, 1854), in which this view is singularly well argued. It is well to halt, however, with a confession, that, while it seems intimated in Holy Scripture, it cannot be proved as revealed. Hence let us reverently say what is said by the Psalmist in Psa. cxxxi. 1, and confess what is written in Deut. xxix. 29. I go so far, only because the words on which this note is a comment seem to authorize inquiry as to the force of "Satan" just there. I state *what seems* the reference, but go no farther. Compare Dan. iv. 35.

III.

The delicacy of feeling here expressed is most honorable to the sentiment of the Church at this period.

Not till St. Bernard's day was it hinted even in the West, that the Blessed Virgin was conceived without taint of original sin; and he rebukes the innovators with a holy indignation. It shocks him that questions were thus raised as to her parents, their *amplexus maritales*, etc.

IV.

Here is testimony to the catechumen system of the primitive Church which appears to me not inconsistent with the period to which it is assigned. No doubt this gradual instruction of the disciple is based upon the example of our Lord Himself, who spoke in parables, and taught "as they were able to hear it." But the *disciplina arcani* was designed chiefly to protect the Church from the profaneness of the heathen, and it fell into desuetude after the Council of Nice.

**Find this and other great works of the
early Church Fathers at
lighthousechristianpublishing.com.**

Archelaus

Our Father who art in heaven, hallowed be
thy name.
Thy kingdom come, Thy will be done, on
earth as it is in heaven.
Give us this day our daily bread and
forgive us our trespasses as we forgive those who
trespass against us.
And lead us not into temptation, but deliver
us from evil, for Thy is the kingdom, the power
and the glory.

Amen

The Acts of the Disposition with the Heresiarch Manes

Hail Mary full of grace, the Lord is with thee. Blessed art thou amongst women and blessed is the fruit of thy womb Jesus. Holy Mary mother of God, pray for us sinners, now and the hour of our death.

www.ingramcontent.com/pod-product-compliance
Lightning Source LLC
Chambersburg PA
CBHW052143070526
44585CB00017B/1953